# THE TIPI

## *Traditional Native American Shelter*

## Adolf Hungrywolf

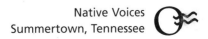
Native Voices
Summertown, Tennessee

Copyright © 2006 by Adolf Hungrywolf

Cover design by Warren Jefferson

Book design by Jerry Lee Hutchens and Gwynelle Dismukes

Published in the United States by

**Native Voices**
Book Publishing Company
P. O. Box 99
Summertown, TN 38483

Printed in Canada

14  13  12  11  10  09  08  07  06          9  8  7  6  5  4  3  2  1

ISBN-13: 978-1-57067-174-6
ISBN-10: 1-57067-174-5

Unless otherwise noted, all photographs are from the collection of Adolf Hungrywolf.

Library of Congress Cataloging-in-Publication Data
Hungrywolf, Adolf, 1944-
  The tipi : Traditional Native American shelter / Adolf
Hungrywolf.
      p. cm.
  "Parts of this book were originally published in 16 small vol-
umes called The good medicine books, copyright by Adolf
Hungrywolf between 1970 and 1979"--T.p. verso.
  Includes bibliographical references and index.
  ISBN-13: 978-1-57067-174-6
  ISBN-10: 1-57067-174-5
  1. Tipis--History--Pictorial works. 2.  Indians of North
America--Dwellings--Pictorial works.  I. Title.
  E98.D9H85 2006
                          2005032983

Printed on recycled paper

The Book Publishing Co. is committed to preserving ancient
forests and natural resources. We have elected to print this
title at Transcontinental on Productolith, which is 10% recycled and
processed chlorine free. As a result of our paper choice, we have
saved the following natural resources:

BOOK
PUBLISHING
COMPANY

11 trees
506 lbs of solid waste
4,588 gallons of water
994 lbs pounds of greenhouse gases
1,845 kw hours of electricity

We are a member of Green Press Initiative. For
more information about Green Press Initiative
visit: www.greenpressinitiative.org     green
                                         press
                                         INITIATIVE

# CONTENTS

# INTRODUCTION TO TIPI LIFE

No structure is more symbolic of North America than the Native conical dwelling best known by the Sioux word "tipi" (also spelled teepee). In fact, few structures in the world have such international fame and recognition, identifiable to people everywhere as the nomadic home of buffalo–hunting North American "Indians."

There can be no definite origin story for a simple structure so ancient as the tipi, though various tales exist among different tribes who lived in them. Primitive peoples in Europe, Asia, and North America used conical structures of poles covered by animal skins. All the well-known tipi-dwelling tribes came to the plains in the last few hundred years from other parts of the continent, some probably bringing along the use of conical lodges, while the rest adopted the idea from them.

The Plains Indian tipi is considered distinct from other conical dwellings because of its adjustable smoke flaps. When properly combined with liner curtains on the inside, the flaps help control air drafts that draw out smoke from the almost-constant wood fires that were a daily part of tipi life in the past.

Excerpts on the following pages will show that tipis were already common among the Plains tribes when the first Europeans met the tribes in the 1500s. Tipis were small then, their furnishings kept meager, since everything had to be hauled by dogs or in backpacks. Long, heavy tipi poles were out of the question for people needing to follow the buffalo.

While tipi life has become thickly shrouded by romantic visions, originally these lodges were made to protect a hardy people in their daily struggles for survival in a harsh and ruthlessly wild life.

The collection of photographs that makes up this volume was gathered over a 40-year period as part of a lifelong project documenting Native cultures and western American history. Many of

A Sioux and his tipi.

*—Photograph by Fiske. Courtesy of the Paul and Theresa Harbaugh Collection.*

the old prints are sadly lacking in written information, but whatever is available has been printed, including the names of photographers and the likely dates. This will serve to present an overall view of tipi life among the various tribes who practiced it on the North American continent.

The written excerpts about tipi life are likewise intended to present in one volume many notes and comments about various ways these traditional dwellings have been used by different tribes. The published works from which they came are listed in 'Sources' near the end of this book. Mostly in the public domain, these are usually out of print and often hard for students to find.

—*Adolf Hungrywolf*

Sioux man on horseback, wearing a trailer of German silver conchos, with another man standing by the tipi.

*—Photo taken at the Fort Laramie camp by Alexander Gardner. Courtesy of the Paul and Theresa Harbaugh Collection.*

1891 on Pine Ridge Agency.

   *—Photograph by Morledge. Courtesy of the Paul and Theresa Harbaugh Collection.*

# Buffalo-Bird-Woman's Narrative

Buffalo-Bird-Woman was born about 1840 in the Hidatsa culture. In 1913 she related this narrative to Gilbert L. Wilson, who published her words in an article entitled "The Horse and Dog in Hidatsa Culture" in *Anthropological Papers of the American Museum of Natural History*.

## Hidatsa Tipi Life

Buffalo-Bird-Woman narrates:

The tent (tipi) we used on this hunt was set up anew at each camp with a framework of freshly cut poles. We always pitched the tent in a rather open place in the timber and on rising ground, a knoll or ridge, where the snow was not so deep. I had brought with me the only hoe in camp and with this I scraped the snow off the ground.

The foundation for the tent framework was of four forked poles, the tops interlocking at the forks. Then an additional half dozen unforked poles were cut with which the circle was completed.

The tent cover consisted of six pieces of skin, each one and one-half or one and one-quarter hides in size, and roughly rectangular in shape. The four corners of each of these rectangular pieces were pierced so the skins could be tied together in a series. Each woman contributed at least once piece of skin toward the completion of the tent. The tent poles were covered in two sections: an upper and a lower series of skins. The lower series was put on first; at intervals, the upper edges of the skins of this series were tied to the tent poles to stay them. The upper series was put on in the same way, but overlapped the lower series like shingles on a house.

As will be noted in figure 76, the door, too, was made to overlap, as shown by the dotted line. To enter the tent, it was necessary to raise this door flap and step over the overlapped portion.

Since the ground was still frozen, tent pins could not be used; instead, small logs were laid along the bottom of the tent upon the edge of the tent skins. For greater security, one or two of these

Indian Village on the 101 Ranch.

*—Photograph by Doubleday. Courtesy of the Paul and Theresa Harbaugh Collection.*

logs was held in place by laying them upon the edge of the tent cover, turning the edge of the cover over the log, either wholly or partly, and inserting a tent pin in the ground. A shallow hole was dug in the hard ground with an ax and the peg driven in, as will be noted to the left of the tent shown in the illustration (fig. 76A). To secure the tent still further, a rawhide thong is tied just above the door, passed around the tent, and then tied to the top of one of the exposed poles (fig. 76B).

In windy weather, a saddle blanket of buffalo belly skin was put up on the windward side of the smoke hole where it was held in place by a forked stick, one prong of the stick being thrust through two apertures cut in the skin (fig. 76C). Its purpose was to prevent the smoke from being driven into the tent by the wind.

During meals we sat in a circle around the fire and facing it, each man with his wife. The food bowls from which we ate were placed before each couple. We had no fixed places in front of the fire, but sat wherever we were inclined.

There was a bed for each couple in the tent, six in all. They were placed head to head and foot to foot … A small log was laid parallel with the wall of the tent and pinned in place by small stakes driven into the ground. Grass was cut with our hoe and heaped on the floor between the log and the wall of the tent. Over the grass were laid two buffalo robes, fur side up. A third was folded, fur side out, for a pillow and laid at the head on a grass cushion. The object of the log was to keep the grass from working out from under the bed and to prevent sparks from setting fire to the grass. The husband always slept on the side toward the fire.

Guns were tied to the tent poles, stock down, each gun over the bed of its owner. Other packages, especially those not easily damaged, such as packages of dried meat, fat, or buffalo intestines, were placed outside the tent along the edge of the tent cover as shown in figure 77.

Gilbert L. Wilson, "The Horse and Dog in Hidatsa Culture," *Anthropological Papers of the American Museum of Natural History*, Vol. XV, Part II, page 243, New York, 1924.

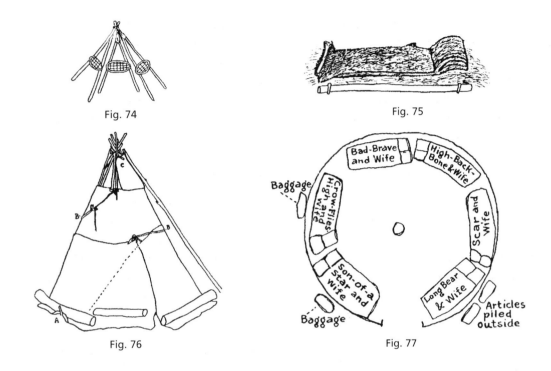

Fig. 74

Fig. 75

Fig. 76

Fig. 77

Fig. 74   Travois stacked for the night.

Fig. 75   Construction of bed used in tent on the hunt.

Fig. 76   The Skin Tent. A, tent pin here driven into the hard ground to prevent log from rolling off the edge of the tent cover; B, rawhide thong drawn around the tent to firm it; C, saddle skin placed as a wind shield to prevent smoke from blowing down the smoke hole.

Fig. 77   Position of the beds within the tent.

# Birth of a Son

Buffalo-Bird-Woman narrates:

About noon, we camped on the sandbar (along the Missouri River). There were about 100 buffalo skin tipis in the camp. When we camped in a good level place it was customary to pitch the tipis in a big circle, and if the wind was calm when we pitched camp, all the tipi doors faced the center of the circle. However, if we were camped along a creek that had a narrow bank, or in any other place where a circle could not be easily formed, the tipis were set up in rows or whatever other arrangement the formation of the land compelled. If there was a stiff wind blowing, a tipi was pitched with the door away from the wind …

Camped thus in a tipi, if a windstorm arose and it became necessary to turn the tipi with the door away from the wind, my husband and I and two or three neighbors, who were invited to help us, could very easily turn it around. Sometimes five persons and sometimes seven or more turned the tipi; the larger number could handle it better, though if there were people enough to hold the foundation poles steady that was sufficient.

First, the pins that held the cover to the ground on the outside were pulled up. Then, we went inside the tipi, picked up the four foundation poles and the one to which the cover was tied and moved the poles and the cover at the same time. The rest of the poles were now shifted about as was necessary. If the five poles were held firmly while they were moved about, there was no danger that the tipi would fall down …

In a Mandan tipi (friends and neighbors of the Hidatsa), a lariat always hung in the center in readiness for a storm. The Mandan three-pole tie was weaker than our Hidatsa four-pole tie and for that reason a lariat was passed around all the poles at the tie. In the Hidatsa tipis this was unnecessary, except in a heavy windstorm, since our poles locked at the top.

Our fireplace was in the center of the tipi on the level ground. Five or six stones were placed around the fire; upon these we roasted meat. We

Part of a circle camp of tipis on the Crow Reservation along the Little Bighorn River. The photo was taken just a few years after the infamous battle with Custer's army was fought near here. Some of the occupants of these tipis no doubt took part, working as army scouts.

A Crow mother is seen helping her child step out of the lodge and into the natural world that surrounds it.

*—Photograph by Rodman Wannamaker.*

never used white stones, for they cracked with the heat. The stones were placed far enough apart so we could roast the thighbone of a buffalo before the fire …

We also roasted a cow udder on a stone before the fire, turning it over to roast it on both sides. We thought a roasted udder full of milk a great delicacy …

The fireplace was surrounded by stones only when wood was scarce and buffalo chips were used for fuel, but when it was abundant the kettle was set directly on the coals and the meat roasted on wooden spits. When we camped on the prairie, however, we could obtain no wood, and made our fire of buffalo chips. In that case, we roasted our meat on stones.

On this trip we used matches to start a fire, but on other trips my father, Small-Ankle, started fire with flint and steel. He carried his fire-making implements in his belt over his right hip. These consisted of a sharp flint, two and one-half inches in diameter, and a semicircle made from an old steel file that was slipped like a ring over the fingers of the right hand. He held the flint in his left hand and under it laid a little piece of dried puffball that had been moistened slightly and rubbed on the surface with gunpowder. A spark struck off by the steel set fire to the puff-ball. Sometimes he used very soft rotten wood instead of a puffball …

When the puffball had caught fire it was placed in a little bunch of shredded dry grass that was then waved back and forth in the air to fan the flame. As I remember, Small-Ankle did not strike the spark upon one whole puffball, but carried in his fire bag a number of these powder-prepared bits of puffball.

In our lodges in Like-a-Fish-Hook village, the fire was smothered at night. If it became extinguished by any accident, the woman went to a neighbor who had a fire and got some coals. We followed the same custom when in camp …

It was known to everyone in the tipi that I was to give birth to a child; so everyone, but me, my father Small-Ankle, and Strikes-Many-Women went away from the tipi. My husband, Son-of-a-Star, went to stay with his brother, Red-Stone. My child was born a little before sunrise.

Son-of-a-Star was in a tent nearby and heard the cry of the child. Later he told me, "I was very happy when I heard the cry of my babe." A piece of an old robe cut out for the purpose was put down on the floor and over it a cloth was laid; the

The old way of carrying a child around the tipi camp, tucked into the mother's robe at the back. The mother holds the front firmly with both hands. These are Crow people.

—*Photograph by Rodman Wannamaker.*

baby was laid on top of this and bound up. On the outside, a soft calfskin was wrapped around him, or sometimes a wildcat skin, but this was done only on the march when there was danger that he would be chilled by the wind. Two wildcat skins and one calfskin were kept for the baby's use, to serve him as a robe does, for an outer dress ...

The morning after the birth of my son, the people began to cross the Missouri River ... Our family crossed in Small-Ankle's bullboat, which we had brought with us. My husband, Son-of-a-Star, helped me in crossing, paddling while I sat in the boat and held my baby. Usually the women paddled the bullboat. Our tent poles, tied in a bundle, were fastened to one of the ribs of the boat and floated behind. In addition, a horse travois and a dog travois were floated over in the same way.

Gilbert L. Wilson, "The Horse and Dog in Hidatsa Culture," *Anthropological Papers of the American Museum of Natural History*, Vol. XV, Part II, page 266, New York, 1924.

*Facing page:* As in this Crow family, traditional tribal mothers were with their children almost constantly, day and night, back when the people practiced tipi life. The young man in the background is inserting the wooden pins for closing up the tipi.

—*Photograph by Rodman Wannamaker.*

*Right:* A Cree tipi for winter camping on the cold northern plains, with a Red River cart parked on the right, circa 1900.

# Gathering Wood

### Buffalo-Bird-Woman narrates:

We always kept wood on hand in the lodge and were careful not to let the pile become depleted. We went out to collect wood when it was convenient. If we had work in the lodge that kept us busy, we might not gather wood for five or six days; but if we had plenty of time, we might go out every day. This was especially true of the winter, when we burned a great deal of wood.

We set out, the four dogs following in single file. As they were hitched to the travois, they never tried to escape or run away; when we stopped, they invariably lay down in the road.

When we reached the timber we cut the wood into lengths two feet two inches long and piled it in the road near the dogs. A load of wood for a dog consisted of a double armful or a little more. It was tied down by the two pack thongs. Besides the travois loads, each woman carried a load on her back, the sticks being cut about two feet six inches, the proper length for our fireplace. The shorter sticks were made up into loads for the travois, because the roads were narrow and the dogs could not turn to avoid trees, as women could. We collected any kind of dry wood, gathering it among the trees, on the sandbar, or in fact wherever we could find it …

For the load a woman carried on her back, she used a pack strap. It had two bands, one going across the shoulders and chest and the other across her forehead. We used the forehead band only to rest our shoulders now and then for a short time. In that case, we let the shoulder band drop and hang loose until we used it again.

I have said that when we came to the woods we piled up our wood, cut in lengths of about two feet two inches, in the path near the dogs, who meanwhile were lying down quietly awaiting their loads. First, we loaded the last dog to arrive, or the one nearest the village. As the dogs always traveled in single file and lay down in the path as soon as we stopped, the last in line lay in the path on the side nearest the village. One of us would approach him, grasp the back of the travois basket, and turn the dog around with his head toward the village. Then we loaded the travois. In like manner, each of the other dogs was turned with his head toward the village.

A daily part of tipi life in the past was the gathering of firewood, usually done by the women and hauled by them in bundles tied over their backs, as these Cheyenne women are doing, circa 1900.

In spite of the fact that the sticks were about four inches shorter, the load, which a dog dragged, contained rather fewer sticks than that which the woman bore on her shoulders. The travois poles were cut flat at the lower end so as to run smoothly over the ground. In summer, a dog travois could not be loaded so heavily as in winter, when it was so much easier for the dog to drag it over the snow-covered ground …

Gilbert L. Wilson, "The Horse and Dog in Hidatsa Culture," *Anthropological Papers of the American Museum of Natural History*, Vol. XV, Part II, New York, 1924.

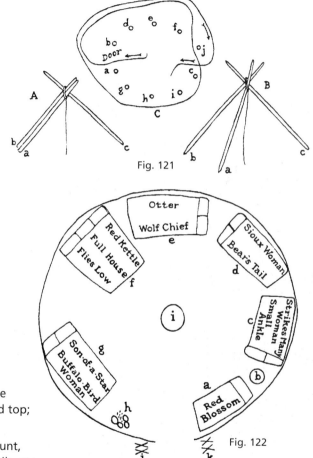

Fig. 121

Fig. 122

Fig. 121   The Mandan Tipi: A, poles tied on the ground; B, the tripod foundation and top; C, the framework.

Fig. 122   Ground plan of tent used on tribal hunt, showing position of household utensils, etc.

Mother crosses a bridge with a child on her back and a dog at her feet.

# Troubled Times

Buffalo-Bird-Woman narrates:

When my son, Goodbird, was about seven years old, word came to the (Hidatsa earth-lodge) village that chicken pox was coming … It was juneberry time and our whole village packed up and went north and camped … The Agency people warned us to keep away from the Missouri River for fear that chicken pox might be brought to us by travelers who came up the river. As out in our country, timber grows only along the rivers, our camp, pitched away from the Missouri, was at a place where we found not very much timber, and what we did find was small in size and scant. Because of this we could not conveniently find tent (tipi) poles … Our camping family was rather large; there were 11 of us in our tent.

We were able, however, to make a tent, or perhaps I should say, shelter, with our dog travois. Three travois were stood up about five feet apart in a line, and each was propped at the top against a forked stick, bound securely to it. Thus each travois and its forked stick support made a tripod. A railing ran along the tops of the three tripods and a second railing ran along the sides just above the baskets. All the baskets of the travois lay toward the weather side of the frame. At each end of this frame two extra poles were bound, one to the travois, the other to the forked stick support. These extra poles were to give the tent a rounded form at the top.

Over the frame thus made (fig. 51) we stretched a tent skin (tipi cover). In figure 52 is shown the tent as it looked at night when closed. In the daytime an entrance was made by raising the two smoke flaps and binding them with thongs to the tops of two sticks to prop them open (fig. 53). These smoke flaps were propped open all day to give air. The rear of the tent is shown in figure 54. As the bottom of the tent was round, this left a rather large margin that lay on the ground (fig. 54A), weighted down with a small log or stone. The floor of the tent was made of tent skins.

There were five beds. Beginning at the left (reckoning Indian fashion) was the bed of my husband, myself, and Goodbird. Although seven years of age, Goodbird still fed at my breast. The second bed toward the right was that of Full-House, Red-Kettle, and Flies-Low … The third bed was that of Charging-Enemy and his wife, Assiniboine-Woman …

We had driven from Like-a-Fish-Hook village in a wagon and there were a number of other wagons in camp. Quite a number of the families had erected tipis. While we were camped here, a terrific storm of rain and wind came up, so severe that many tipis were blown down and wagons were overturned; but our shelter withstood the storm safely. During the worst of the wind, we held the frame firmly, the better to withstand the wind.

Gilbert L. Wilson, "The Horse and Dog in Hidatsa Culture," *Anthropological Papers of the American Museum of Natural History*, Vol. XV, Part II, page 221, New York, 1924.

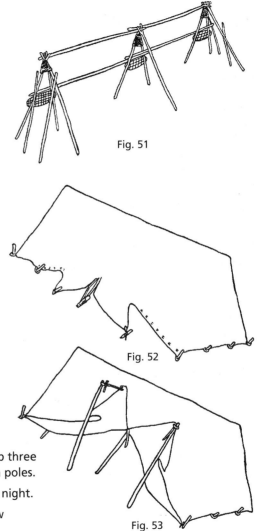

Fig. 51

Fig. 52

Fig. 53

Fig. 51   Frame for shelter made by setting up three dog travois and adding several extra poles.

Fig. 52   The shelter with flaps closed for the night.

Fig. 53   The shelter with flaps raised to allow circulation of air.

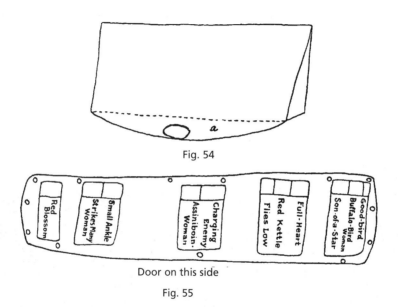

Fig. 54

Door on this side

Fig. 55

Fig. 54   Rear of shelter tent, with excess of cover
weighted down with a stone.

Fig. 55   Interior sleeping arrangements in a travois
shelter tent.

26

Tipis, tents, wagons, and horses make up this Mandan camp along the Missouri River near Fort Berthold, North Dakota, in 1905.

In the foothills of the Canadian Rockies, near Calgary, Alberta, this well-dressed young Sarcee woman is seen on her buffalo pony by her family lodge, circa 1890. The tripod next to her horse holds rawhide bags guarding sacred articles, while the storage rack farther back consists of travois frames balanced together. These A-shaped rigs were the trailers of traditional tipi life, carrying the kids and household baggage.

*—Photograph by C. W. Mathers.*

Two mothers transport their children by horse-drawn travois.

# Travois

Buffalo-Bird-Woman narrates:

The pony carrying the six poles also carried the tent skin. When the tent was struck, the cover was untied from the rear pole and laid on the ground, weather side up (fig. 106A). Then it was folded over once, weather side in (fig. 106B) and the smoke hole end was folded once over (fig. 106C). Each end of the package was successively folded over twice (fig. 106D); the result is shown in figure 106E. Now the two sides, A and B, are folded together and each end is folded twice toward the center (fig. 107F). A lariat is then passed around three times and tied (fig. 107G) and the tent swung to the horse's back. Then the free end of the lariat (fig. 107G, E) was carried under the horse's belly and tied on the horse. As has already been said, each of the tent poles had a hole at the smaller end through which a thong was drawn.

The larger ends of the poles dragged loosely on the ground, spread [in a] fan shape. Sometimes one of these tent poles broke where it was pierced for drawing through the thong. In that case, a slight groove was cut into the pole as a substitute …

As the tent cover lay on the horse, it made a load on either side of the animal, 12 inches thick, 26 inches long, and 24 inches wide, while the connecting portion that passed over the saddle was about 18 inches long … When a pony carried a tent cover, no boy or older person ever rode it.

Gilbert L. Wilson, "The Horse and Dog in Hidatsa Culture," *Anthropological Papers of the American Museum of Natural History*, Vol. XV, Part II, page 278, New York, 1924.

# On the Move

Transporting a lodge and its contents in 1833, reported by Maximilian, Prince of Wied, *Travels in the Interior of North America*, London, 1843.

Preparation for their transportation is made in the following manner: The poles of the lodges, which are from 20 to 35 feet in length, are divided, the small ends being lashed together and secured to the shoulders of the horse, allowing the butt-ends to drag upon the ground on either side; just behind the horse are secured to cross-pieces, to keep the poles in their respective places, and upon which are placed the lodge and domestic furniture. This also serves for the safe transportation of the children and infirm unable to ride on horseback—the lodge being folded so as to allow two or more to ride securely.

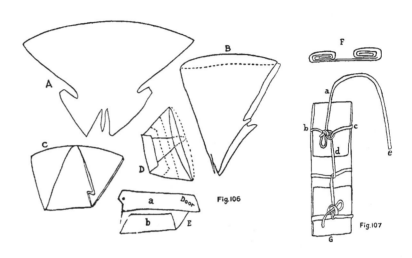

Fig. 106   Method of folding a tent cover in preparation for loading.

Fig. 107   A tent cover tied ready for loading.

The horses dragging this burden—often of 300 pounds—are also ridden by the squaws, with a child astride behind, and one in her arms, embracing a favorite young pup.

David I. Bushnell, Jr., "Villages of the Algonquin, Siouan, and Caddoan Tribes West of the Mississippi," *Bulletin of the Bureau of American Ethnology* (Bulletin 77), page 30, Smithsonian Institution, Washington, DC, 1922.

Turning forests into farms in Northern Alberta inspired some novel ideas, including the taming of this poor young moose, trained to haul loads with harness and modified travois. —*C.W. Mathers photo. Ernest Brown Collection.*

Traveling by horse-drawn travois.

# Skin Tents

**Buffalo-Bird-Woman narrates:**

The buffalo skin tent used by our family during this hunt was of my own construction. The hides obtained during a summer hunt were used for tent skins, for parfleches, bags, and rawhide ropes, but never for robes; while those obtained on the winter hunt were tanned for use as robes, bed coverlets, bedding, and winter moccasins. This was our old-time custom. I never knew of any who used winter hides for a tent cover.

The tent we carried with us on this hunt was of 13 large cow skins that my husband had brought in. I scraped the skins clean, taking off every little bit of flesh that still clung to them, dried them, removed the hair with an elk horn scraper, oiled them, and hung them in the sun. To tan a skin, I soaked it in water overnight and the process was completed by evening of the next day. When the skins were tanned and ready, I cut them myself. Cutting tent skins was a sacred office and followed as a profession, so that not everyone in camp could cut the skins of a tent cover.

Having staked a raw deer hide to the ground, hair side down, this Cheyenne woman is scraping the flesh and fat with a steel blade attached to an L-shaped piece of elk horn.

34

When the skins had been cut, a party of about nine women was invited in to sew the tent for me. For this work, I gave them a feast consisting of one wooden bowl full of corn balls, one kettle full of boiled sweet corn, one kettle full of dried buffalo meat, one panful of biscuits, and one kettle full of coffee. In case a tent cutter was hired in addition, special food had to be prepared for her.

The tent poles were of pine (spruce) brought to the village by visiting Crow. In spite of the fact that they did not grow on our reservation, we always had a great many of these poles. They lasted a long time. There were fifteen poles to our tent, including the two that upheld the smoke hole flaps. The tent door was an old cloth blanket. On the hunt, the tent door was often made of a deerskin-hung fur inside so that whenever anyone went out of the tent, the fur of the door skin fell smooth against the head and body. For this reason, the fur was hung head up.

Gilbert L. Wilson, "The Horse and Dog in Hidatsa Culture," *Anthropological Papers of the American Museum of Natural History*, Vol. XV, Part II, page 291, New York, 1924.

Tanning a deer hide by her lodge, this Cheyenne woman has a steel scythe blade tied to an upright pole to help her soften the hide and remove all its hair.
—*Photograph by George Bird Grinnell.*

35

# Hunting Camp

Wolf-Chief (brother of Buffalo-Bird-Woman) describes a camp made when just he and his father went hunting on horseback with dog and travois, about 1866.

We reached the camping place and dismounted. My father untied our dog from the travois. He was a good dog and not very tired. As soon as the travois was removed, he rolled in the snow, getting up and shaking his hide, but not barking. We also unloaded our horses, but did not hobble them. "They are tired and will not stray far," said my father. We had made about 20 miles that day.

Our horses attended to, my father began putting up the frame of our tent. He raised the travois, stayed it against a forked pole, and against these leaned other poles, which he brought from the timber. It was about six feet high and I remember that I had to stoop a little as I stood within by the fireplace. It was covered with three pieces of old tent skin, two at the front and one at the back. My father pierced holes in the skins with his knife and through the holes drew thongs to lace the skins together. At the front of the tent, the edges of the upper skin did not meet, but the space thus left open was filled in by the netted thongs of the travois basket. The door was under the travois basket. Its covering was a saddle skin with the head cut off, hanging fur side in. The tent was tied in front in two places.

We went to bed, my father on the north side of the tent, I on the south. My dog slept at my side. Our saddles were laid against the tent wall. In this case, we did not use tent pins or stones to hold down the edge of the tent covering; it merely hung to the ground. The floor of our tent had been scraped free of snow with our hoe. We had brought the hoe with us to scrape the snow from our camping places. Our guns lay near us. "Put your gun beside you," my father had said to me. "If enemies fire at our tent, pay no attention to anything, but seize your gun." I laid my gun between myself and the skin covering of the tent with the barrel pointing in the same direction as my head. We had a small fire outside our tent. We carried with us one drinking cup.

Gilbert L. Wilson, "The Horse and Dog in Hidatsa Culture," *Anthropological Papers of the American Museum of Natural History*, Vol. XV, Part II, page 299, New York, 1924.

A Cheyenne woman is fleshing the cowhide she has staked hair side down in a tipi camp on the prairie, circa 1895. —*Photograph by George Bird Grinnell.*

# Snow Storm

Wolf-Chief narrates:

We camped at night on a hill and Small-Ankle made bone grease. A storm came up and it began to snow. "We must move our camp down into the timber," said my father. "Our tent may blow over up here." The next day we moved our tent down in a coulee out of the wind and pitched it in a place near a big tree where it was protected by some bushes. It snowed all day. In the evening it was still snowing, but we went back to our meat pile near our former camp on the hill to take our meat back to our tent. Snow was still falling when we went to bed. I slept that night on the west side with my head toward the rear of the tent. The tent door was toward the south.

Our tent poles were small and not heavy enough to support the weight of the snow. I do not know how it happened, but apparently the snow on the side of the hill above us on the west drifted and came down upon me. My father awoke during the night to find the tent giving way and weighted down with the snow. The space inside the tent was reduced almost to nothing. He sprang across and found me under the snow, unconscious. He carried me to the farther side of the tent, sang a mystery song, and felt my heart. Like one in a dream, I heard him singing. Gradually, my senses returned. "Are you alive again!" cried my father. "Yes," I answered, my breath coming in gasps, as I sat up.

My father held me in his arms, as I sat on the ground, but I was able to sit upright only by leaning my head against the tent wall. The wall was icy cold, but I could not sit up otherwise. "I once heard," said my father, "of a tent being covered with snow. The people inside hit the walls of the tent with their hands and kept the snow from crushing it to the ground." He struck the tent wall repeatedly at one side, driving back the snow and packing it; after a while he had quite a space cleared. "You sit here," my father said. I moved over to the side where he had been working and he attacked the other side of the tent. At last, he had the tent restored to something like its normal shape …

My father now dug with the hoe into the snow at the door and as he dug I kept shoving the snow back into the lodge. We both wore our mittens, but my father covered his head with a saddle skin set over his hair like a cap. He cut holes in the edges of the saddle skin where they overlapped and struck a stick through to skewer the edges together. This saddle skin cap prevented the snow from falling on his bare head, as he was digging a tunnel through the snowdrift … We continued to work in this manner and finally I broke through the drift about 18 feet from the tent. We had worked on our knees and dug a tunnel high enough to kneel in; the snow was at least 10 feet deep …

When I had tunneled through the snow, my dog met me at the mouth of the tunnel. While we were still in the tent, my father and I heard a noise overhead that we thought was made by a ghost, but it was only my dog on the snowdrift above us.

We remained at this spot the rest of that day and through the night, digging the tunnel out to the ground to reach our tent.

We cut the sinews used to sew the tent skins together and in this way removed the cover, piece by piece. We abandoned the poles.

Gilbert L. Wilson, "The Horse and Dog in Hidatsa Culture," *Anthropological Papers of the American Museum of Natural History*, Vol. XV, Part II, page 307, New York, 1924.

# Buffalo Hides

Told by Maxi'diwiac in 1912:

I have said that we made the threshing the drying stage (out in the garden), of an old tent (tipi) cover.

Buffalo hides that we wanted to use for making tent covers were taken in the spring when the buffaloes shed their hair and their skins are thin. The skin tent cover that we then made would be used all that summer; and the next winter, perhaps, we would begin to cut it up for moccasins. The following spring, again, we could take more buffalo hides and make another tent cover.

Not all families renewed a tent so often. Some families used a tent two years, and some even a much longer time; but many families used a tent cover but a single season. It was a very usual thing for the women of a family to make a new tent cover in the spring.

Old tent covers, as I have said, were cut up for moccasins, or they were put to other uses. There was always a good deal of need about the lodge for skins that had been scraped bare of hair; and the skins in a tent cover were, of course, of this kind. Every bed in the earth lodge, in old times, was covered with an old tent cover.

Skins needed in threshing time were partly of these bed covers, taken down from the beds. Often the piece of an old tent cover from which we had been cutting moccasins would be brought out and used. Then we commonly had other buffalo hides, scraped bare of hair, stored in the lodge, ready for any use.

Gilbert L. Wilson, "Agriculture of the Hidatsa Indians—An Indian Interpretation," *Studies in Social Sciences*, No. 9, page 118, University of Minnesota, Minneapolis, 1917.

Combining the nomadic ways of tipi living with the settled peace on reservations, many traditional families continued to develop their ceremonial and material cultures, even after the so-called old days were over. The sunshade and meat drying rack in the foreground also shelter a table and chair, along with a grinding wheel and sundry buckets. Variations of this scene still take place across the plains, even in this day and age.

# Peyote Tipi

These tales were collected in ... 1927 from Kiowa met haphazardly in Oklahoma over the sixty miles or so from Anadarko to Hobart ... From the houses thus wished on them (by the government agent) and which are for the most part uncared for and exceedingly disorderly, families often escape to tent or tipi in the summer ...

Alongside the stove-warmed tent, Sendema (a noted Kiowa elder of the period) had set up the peyote tipi of which she was the proud owner (the family also owned another tipi that had been made by their paternal great-aunt), beautifully stretched over its 20 cedar poles, and one night I found her roasting meat on the forked stick inclined over the neatly cut circular fire hole the meat dripped into as the embers fell from the tips of the fire sticks laid above. The fire should have been lit with a spark from two flints caught in bark fiber and kept in the horn of a young buffalo, and the meat—it should have been a buffalo steak! But only those "strong for peyote," the cult with which old ways are today associated, make fire by flint nowadays, and the meat came from the butcher shop of Anadarko, the family having just returned from their Saturday afternoon in town where they hung about the stores and went to the "picture" and made acquaintances.

Elsie Clews Parsons, "Kiowa Tales," *American Folklore Society Memoir* 22. New York, 1929.

Quanah Parker and one of his wives. Quanah was chief of the Quahadi Comanche, the last band to surrender in the southern plains war of 1874–1875. Quanah Parker helped integrate Christian elements with the traditional use of peyote, and insisted that women be included in the ceremonies.

—*Courtesy of the Paul and Theresa Harbaugh Collection.*

# Medicine Tipi

Pit'dogede, or Feathers-Standing-Inside, or Mrs. Frank Bosu, then aged 63, narrates:

When I was a little girl and we were camping near my grandfather Anso'te, a cyclone came. People called out to Anso'te to make medicine … He took down the "taime" (a revered Kiowa medicine, kept outside behind the tipi in the daytime) lest it be thrown down (which would be considered a bad sign for the tribe). He put the cord attached to "taime" around his neck, and carried it in his arms. Wearing a buffalo robe, buffalo moccasins, he held out his buffalo robe from his body, both arms widespread, and ran around his tipi four times, and sat down at the tipi entrance; again he did this. He spoke to Red Horse (a Kiowa spiritual being), holding out his arms. It hailed and rained. Not a tipi was left standing, except one little one. Mother shoved us children under the beds (raised on poles four to six inches above the ground). It would have been worse had not Anso'te made his medicine.

Elsie Clews Parsons, "Kiowa Tales," *American Folklore Society Memoir* 22. New York, 1929.

# Tipi Conjuring

Frank Bosu narrates:

The Apache have medicine to find a lost horse. The old man who had it died last week. Formerly the Kiowa, too, had this medicine. A small buffalo skin tipi was set up inside of the big tipi. People sat quietly and voices came from inside this small tipi. Four pipes lay on the ground. The medicine man said, "I am calling the old people long since dead." "Ha! Ha! Yes! Yes!" "You smoke!" "What do you want?" "A horse is lost." "Of what color?" The medicine man tells its color. "Yes, I see it." "Where?" "Over there." "Drive it this way! … So in the morning I find it."

Elsie Clews Parsons, "Kiowa Tales," *American Folklore Society Memoir* 22. New York, 1929.

"Tipi creeping" was probably known by the young plainsman in the foreground, though unmarried girls in most tribes were carefully guarded. Sneaking into someone else's tipi at night was a common, though dangerous, venture back when lodge owners kept weapons handy to defend against marauding enemies. These small lodges with their short poles look like part of a hunting camp, rather than a powwow or ceremonial gathering. Although the man has on a coat and hat, the weather must have been warm since all the lodges have their covers raised at the bottom.

# Kiowa Hand Game

Towa'gya, tipi sinde game, or hand game. The crier would call out in the evening, "Where are we going to have a big hand game tonight?" The chief would call out in answer, "In my tipi!"… Ten men to each side sit in two lines facing each other, on north and south sides of the tipi.

The women come in and sit behind the side they favor. Use a piece of bone to hide in their hand, hold out both fists. Start with man in the centre of the line. Man opposite has to guess in which hand is the bone. If he thinks it is in the hand to the west he raises his hand to the west, his hand doubled up, with the thumb pointing to the west, similarly for the hand to the east, he points the thumb of his east side hand to the east. Four judges sit on the west side with four tally sticks in front of each line of players. The score place is in the northwest corner. The method of scoring is somewhat complicated, and for lack of time I did not record it.

Both sides sing:

> In winter … going to sleep … I like it
> Where it is … Where it is …
> In winter … going to sleep … I like it
> You have found it … You not find it, I have
>   another hand.

Elsie Clews Parsons, "Kiowa Tales," *American Folklore Society Memoir* 22. New York, 1929.

These Cheyenne women are seen playing the traditional dice game
inside their tipi, circa 1900.

# Young Couple's First Tipi

**Pit'dogede narrates:**

I, his mother, and perhaps my sister with me, will go and talk to the girl's people. Later we give to them four horses and nice blankets and buckskin and moccasins. The girl's people gather together household utensils to give to us, also four horses …

The girl will take the boy to visit her people. After a while she asks him, "Where are we going to live, with your folks or my folks?" He says, "I guess we will stay in my mother's house. Then when we get tired of it there, we will go to your home." They may stay one year or so with his people, and then go to her people. After that they will make their own living, cook their own meals, have their own horses, and their own tipi. Their tipi may be near that of the boy's people or of the girl's people, if all live in the same camp. If the families are living in different camps, they will put up their tipi in the camp of the girl's people.

Elsie Clews Parsons, "Kiowa Tales," *American Folklore Society Memoir* 22. New York, 1929.

## Grandma's Tipi

**Pit'dogede narrates:**

My grandmother lived alone in a little tipi near ours. We children would stay with her during the day, and one of us would sleep with her. She was very old; she would creep about, sometimes get lost, and we would have to find her and bring her back. She was thinking all the time of how she used to live. She would tear up her blanket to make a rope to go hunting. Then she would get a sack and put everything around her into it—at that time she was moving camp. "My son is coming with some buffalo meat," she would say. Sometimes she would put down her head to be loused. "Look for my buffalo!" she would say for this. I did not want to do this, and she would kick me and call to my mother, "Mata! (girl)" she called. My mother would come and laugh. I did not like to sleep with her, she was so shrunken and skinny and bony. I wonder if I am going to be that way, I would say to myself. Pretty bad! No, I won't be that way.

Tipi life in a Rocky Mountain meadow in 1974. This has been the dream life of many young couples who dread the thought of settling down to raise children in the crowded and polluted cities.

—*Photograph by Adolf Hungrywolf.*

*Source, facing page:* Elsie Clews Parsons, "Kiowa Tales," *American Folklore Society Memoir* 22. New York, 1929.

# Ute tipis

The Utes lived in tipis of skin in winter, and in brush shelters made by placing brush over a frame of poles in summer. Elk skin was in common use as a tipi covering, but buffalo skin was preferred when it was obtainable ...

Helen Sloan Daniels, *The Ute Indians of Southwestern Colorado*, Durango Public Library Museum Project, page 99, Durango, Colorado, 1941.

*Facing page:* A mountain camp at Los Pinos, Colorado, in 1874, nearly 10 years before the Ute people were to make their final buffalo hunts.

—*Photograph by William H. Jackson.*

A well-dressed warrior on horseback, photographed at Los Pinos, Colorado, during the final years of a buffalo hunting lifestyle, while the people were still partly nomadic. Ute tipis were considered more plain than those of most other tribes. The one at left has no earflaps, doesn't close fully at the front, and is held up by very skimpy poles. The Utes used other types of traditional shelters as well.

—*Photograph by William H. Jackson.*

*Facing page:* An old Ojibwa man standing by a hunting lodge in eastern Canada shows off his traditional hooded coat of wild rabbit skins, circa 1920.

—*Courtesy of the National Museum of Canada.*

*Source, facing page:* David I. Bushnell, Jr., "Villages of the Algonquin, Siouan, and Caddoan Tribes West of the Mississippi," *Bulletin of the Bureau of American Ethnology* (Bulletin 77), page 7, Smithsonian Institution, Washington, DC, 1922.

# Lodge Forms

The villages as well as the separate structures reared by the many tribes who formerly occupied the region treated in the present work presented marked characteristics, causing them to be easily identified by the early travelers through the wilderness of a century ago. The mat and bark covered wigwam predominated among the Algonquin tribes of the north, although certain members of this great linguistic family also used the skin tipi so typical of the Siouan tribes of the plains, while some of the latter stock constructed the earth lodge similar to that erected by the Caddoan tribes. Thus it will be understood that no one group occupied habitations of a single form to the exclusion of all others, and again practically all the tribes had two or more types of dwellings that were reared and used under different conditions, some forming their permanent villages, others being easily removed and transported, serving as their shelters during long journeys in search of the buffalo.

# Ojibwa Bark Lodges

Recorded in 1804 by fur trader Peter Grant of the North-West Company.

Their tents are constructed with slender long poles, erected in the form of a cone and covered with the rind of the birch tree. The general diameter of the base is about 15 feet, the fireplace exactly in the middle, and the remainder of the area, with the exception of a small place for the hearth, is carefully covered with the branches of the pine or cedar tree, over which some bearskins and old blankets are spread, for sitting and sleeping. A small aperture is left in which a bearskin is hung in lieu of a door, and a space is left open at the top, which answers the purpose of window and chimney. In stormy weather the smoke would be intolerable, but this inconvenience is easily removed by contracting or shifting the aperture at top according to the point from which the wind blows. It is impossible to walk, or even to stand upright, in their miserable habitations, except directly around the fireplace. The men sit generally with their legs stretched before them, but the women have theirs folded backwards, inclined a little to the left side, and can comfortably remain the whole day in those attitudes, when the weather is too bad for remaining out-of-doors. In fine weather they are very fond of basking in the sun.

When the family is very large, or when several families live together, the dimensions of their tents are, of course, in proportion and of different forms. Some of these spacious habitations resemble the roof of a barn, with small openings at each end for doors, and the whole length of the ridge is left uncovered at top for the smoke and light.

David I. Bushnell, Jr., "Villages of the Algonquin, Siouan, and Caddoan Tribes West of the Mississippi," *Bulletin of the Bureau of American Ethnology* (Bulletin 77), page 9, Smithsonian Institution, Washington, DC, 1922.

An Ojibwa winter hunting lodge, or wigwam, seen in eastern Canada, circa 1925.

—*Courtesy of the National Museum of Canada.*

# The Lodge of an Ojibwa Hunter

Recorded in 1858 by Henry Youle Hind, while traveling with the Assiniboine and Saskatchewan Exploring Expedition.

His birch-bark tent was roomy and clean. Thirteen persons including children squatted round the fire in the centre. On the floor some excellent matting was laid upon spruce boughs for the strangers; the squaws squatted on the bare ground, the father of the family on an old buffalo robe. Attached to the poles of the tent were a gun, bows and arrows, a spear, and some mink skins. Suspended on crosspieces over the fire were fishing nets and floats, clothes, and a bunch of the bearberry to mix with tobacco for the manufacture of kinni-kinnik.

David I. Bushnell, Jr., "Villages of the Algonquin, Siouan, and Caddoan Tribes West of the Mississippi," *Bulletin of the Bureau of American Ethnology* (Bulletin 77), page 12, Smithsonian Institution, Washington, DC, 1922.

## Ojibwa Lodge Fire

Around the fire in the center, and at a distance of perhaps two feet from it, are placed sticks as large as one's arm, in a square form, guarding the fire; and it is a matter of etiquette not to put one's feet nearer the fire than that boundary. One or more pots or kettles are hung over the fire on the crotch of a sapling. In the sides of the wigwam are stowed all clothing, food, cooking utensils, and other property of the family.

David I. Bushnell, Jr., "Villages of the Algonquin, Siouan, and Caddoan Tribes West of the Mississippi," *Bulletin of the Bureau of American Ethnology* (Bulletin 77), page 11, Smithsonian Institution, Washington, DC, 1922.

The "Summer Camp" is the generic title given to this scene. It looks like art photographer Roland Reed got a few old timers to get out sacred headdresses and old beadwork for this posed photo. He also added these comments: "In summer the Ojibway Indians (often called Chippewa) pitched their teepees or wigwams on the lake shores so they could beach their canoes conveniently and also be close to their fishing grounds, rice fields, etc. A visitor has just arrived."

# Ojibwa Medicine Lodge

Record of Paul Kane's visit to an Ojibwa "medicine lodge" of the sacred "mide" society near Lake Winnipeg in 1846.

It was rather an oblong structure, composed of poles bent in the form of an arch, and both ends forced into the ground, so as to form, when completed, a long arched chamber, protected from the weather by a covering of birch bark …

On my first entrance … I found four men, who appeared to be chiefs, sitting upon mats spread upon the ground, gesticulating … and keeping time to the beating of a drum. Something apparently of a sacred nature was covered up in the centre of the group, which I was not allowed to see … The interior of their lodge or sanctuary was hung round with mats constructed with rushes, to which were attached various offerings …

David I. Bushnell, Jr., "Villages of the Algonquin, Siouan, and Caddoan Tribes West of the Mississippi," *Bulletin of the Bureau of American Ethnology* (Bulletin 77), page 13, Smithsonian Institution, Washington, DC, 1922.

# Emergency Hide Lodge

Remembered by John Tanner from his 30-year captivity among the Ojibwa in the early 1800s.

In bad weather we used to make a little lodge, and cover it with three or four fresh buffalo hides, and these being soon frozen, made a strong shelter from wind and snow. In calm weather, we commonly encamped with no other covering than our blankets.

David I. Bushnell, Jr., "Villages of the Algonquin, Siouan, and Caddoan Tribes West of the Mississippi," *Bulletin of the Bureau of American Ethnology* (Bulletin 77), page 13, Smithsonian Institution, Washington, DC, 1922.

# Tipis of the Plains

Camp on the Plains.

# Ancient Stone Tipi Rings

The Plains Crees, in the day of their power and pride, had erected large skin tents and strengthened them with rings of stones placed round the base. These circular remains were 25 feet in diameter, the stones or boulders being about one foot in circumference. They wore the aspect of great antiquity, being partially covered with soil and grass.

David I. Bushnell, Jr., "Villages of the Algonquin, Siouan, and Caddoan Tribes West of the Mississippi," *Bulletin of the Bureau of American Ethnology* (Bulletin 77), page 20, Smithsonian Institution, Washington, DC, 1922.

Several generations of Cree lived together in the two large tipis (plus a small one for playing and cooking) seen here on the northern plains around 1900, when several small groups like this still roamed nomadically.

A young Cree couple with child stands posed in front of their small tipi camp on the northern plains, circa 1900.

Cree fishing camp in northern Alberta, circa 1900.

—*Photograph by Edward S. Curtis.*

Two young warriors by their tipi camp in the "bush" of northern Alberta soon after the war days had ended, circa 1890. —*Photograph by C. W. Mathers, Ernest Brown Studio. Courtesy of the Bob Scriver Collection.*

A nomadic tipi camp of Cree buffalo hunters is seen near the Cypress Hills of southern Alberta in 1878, as buffalo hunting was coming to an end. The people in this camp really knew tipi life, the only kind of life they had. —*Courtesy of the Bob Scriver Collection.*

A Cree woman in calico dress cooks over an open fire near her tipi, while three boys dressed in blanket coats and moccasins stand nearby. Behind them was the family's main transportation, a two-wheeled Red River cart.

—*Photograph by Thomas H. Mather.*

Fine Day was a noted chief of the Sweetgrass Cree at Battleford, Saskatchewan, a former warrior, medicine man, and wise counselor. He stands here smiling, holding his little granddaughter, and wearing a beaded vest and his sacred horned weasel headdress. His tipi is decorated with drawings and feather plumes as directed in his dreams. This was at a tribal Sun Dance camp in June 1911.

*—Photograph by David Mandelbaum.*

The transition period for traditional Cree life is shown by this couple—dressed in modern clothing yet still wearing long braids, standing by their canvas tent with a tipi in the background. Photograph taken at Hobbema, Alberta, in 1911.

—*Photograph by David Mandelbaum.*

A Cree hunting camp on the northern plains, circa 1900.

*—Photograph by Edward S. Curtis.*

# Cheyenne Lodges

While living in the vicinity of the Minnesota (River) the villages and camps of the Cheyenne undoubtedly resembled those of the Sioux of later days—the conical skin-covered lodge, or possibly the mat or bark structure of the timber people, as used by the Ojibway and others. But during the same period it is evident other bands of the tribe lived quite a distance westward, probably on the banks of the Missouri, and there the habitations were the permanent earth lodge, similar to those of the Pawnee, Mandan, and other Missouri Valley tribes.

Wrapped in his blanket and seated on the ground by his tipi, this Cheyenne elder raises his pipe in respect to the spirits with whom he speaks in his prayer. Men favored this style of wearing a robe, with only one shoulder covered to leave the other arm free.

—*Photograph by George Bird Grinnell.*

*Facing page:* Women demonstrate how to set up a tipi in this 1911 photograph taken on the Cheyenne Agency, South Dakota.

—*Photograph by Cundill, courtesy of the Paul and Theresa Harbaugh Collection.*

*Source, facing page:* David I. Bushnell, Jr., "Villages of the Algonquin, Siouan, and Caddoan Tribes West of the Mississippi," *Bulletin of the Bureau of American Ethnology* (Bulletin 77), page 22, Smithsonian Institution, Washington, DC, 1922.

The transition era in North America's Native history included long periods of heavy proselytizing for "Native souls" by the various mainstream religions. This scene is an example, taken in Oklahoma, circa 1910. The preachers have come to visit a couple of traditional southern Cheyenne women seen in front of their tipi. To translate, and perhaps help persuade, they have brought two younger Native women dressed in modern fashion—old enough to have spent their childhood in tipis like this, but gone to see what else the world had to offer.

Smoking a pipe next to the doorway of her tipi is noted Cheyenne elder Bead Woman, circa 1895.

—*Photograph by George Bird Grinnell.*

A simple sunshade protects these Cheyenne women while they cut meat for drying. Several sliced sheets are already hanging above them. —*Photograph by George Bird Grinnell.*

Wearing her blanket low so as to leave the arms free for working, this Cheyenne woman is crushing chokecherries with a stone mortar and pestle in front of her tipi, circa 1900. The crushed fruit will be stored in the rawhide envelope bag lying next to her.

A well-dressed young Cheyenne man holds up his wrapped blanket with one hand while playing the traditional wheel and arrow game at the edge of camp, circa 1895.

—*Photograph by George Bird Grinnell.*

A Cheyenne camp of tipis and tents seen in Oklahoma, circa 1915. Most tribes set up their tipis to face the rising sun in the east, but various factors could change that, as seen here with the closest tipi facing opposite its two neighbors. The tipis of some tribes had ribbons and strips of cloth hanging from the tips of their poles for decoration and to help keep rainwater from running down inside.

Part of a nomadic Cheyenne hunting camp that includes a short, squat tipi and a covered wagon behind, circa 1915.

Photograph shows the famous Treaty Council of 1869, when the Sioux were "given" the Black Hills, which was later stolen from them again. This treaty resulted in the closing of the Boseman Trail. The white man in the middle smoking a pipe is one of the government's commissioners. To his left is Old Man Afraid of His Horses, hereditary chief of the Oglalla Sioux and the main chief at this gathering. He is not wearing a shirt. Near him are General William S. Harney and General William Sheridan.

—*Photograph taken at Fort Laramie by Alexander Gardner. Courtesy of the Paul and Theresa Harbaugh Collection.*

Cheyenne medicine lodges on the Yellowstone, 1877, featuring a tipi with painted designs and scalps hanging from a pole. A buffalo skull, for ceremonial use, lies on the ground.

—*Photograph by S. J. Morrow, Yankton, Dakota Territory. Courtesy of the Paul and Theresa Harbaugh Collection.*

# Lakota Lodges

As will be shown in the sketches of the dwellings and other structures of the Dakota tribes, those who lived in the timbered region occupying much of the present state of Minnesota erected the (wigwam) type of habitation characteristic of the region, but in the villages along the Minnesota, both bark- and skin-covered lodges were in use, and the more western villages were formed exclusively of the latter type, the conical skin tipi of the plains.

David I. Bushnell, Jr., "Villages of the Algonquin, Siouan, and Caddoan Tribes West of the Mississippi," *Bulletin of the Bureau of American Ethnology* (Bulletin 77), page 44, Smithsonian Institution, Washington, DC, 1922.

Sitting Bull's camp at Fort Randall, Dakota Territory. This was when Sitting Bull was a prisoner of war after the 1881 surrender.

*—Photograph by W. R. Cross. Courtesy of the Paul and Theresa Harbaugh Collection.*

The title on this sepia-toned postcard from the 1920s reads, "Big Indian Village Pow Wow," but the Sioux tipi camp was probably set up for a movie, with a big crowd of mounted warriors in the center, while many more on foot are gathered around. The people of that era would have enjoyed getting paid to set up their tipis, being given free food, and earning a few more dollars for dressing in their best clothing. Some of the tipis are way up on the hillside, adding scope to this photo, but sitting on ground so sloped that anyone trying to sleep in one of them would have been in for some nighttime tumbling.     —*Photograph courtesy of the Azusa Card Collection.*

# Little Raven

Visit to the Sioux village of Little Raven, near present-day St. Paul, Minnesota, by E.S. Seymour in 1849, from *Sketches of Minnesota*, New York, 1850.

During the time I visited them, the Indians were living in skin lodges, such as they use during the winter and when traveling. These are formed of long, slender poles, stuck in the ground, in a circle of about eight feet in diameter, and united at the top, and covered with the raw hide of the buffalo, having the hair scraped off ... During the summer they live in bark houses, which are more spacious, and when seen from a distance, resemble, in form and appearance, the log cabins of the whites. When passing in sight of the village, a few days afterwards, I noticed they had removed their skin lodges and erected their bark houses. The population of this village ... is from 250 to 300 souls.

(Entering a small skin covered lodge, he noted:) An iron kettle, suspended in the center, over a fire, forms the principal cooking utensil. Blankets spread around on the ground were used as seats and beds.

David I. Bushnell, Jr., "Villages of the Algonquin, Siouan, and Caddoan Tribes West of the Mississippi," *Bulletin of the Bureau of American Ethnology* (Bulletin 77), page 50, Smithsonian Institution, Washington, DC, 1922.

Minnesota tipis. —*Courtesy of the Paul and Theresa Harbaugh Collection.*

# Medicine Bags

Every medicine man had a bag or case in which he kept his supply of herbs and the articles used by him in treating the sick. In some instances the outer case was of decorated rawhide. A man's medicine bag was hung on a pole outside the lodge and usually brought in at night; it was often "incensed" with burning sweetgrass. It was believed that the presence of "the wrong kind of person" in the lodge would affect the efficacy of the medicine, and that if it were exposed to such influence for any considerable time its power would be entirely destroyed.

Frances Densmore, "Teton Sioux Music,"
*Bulletin of the Bureau of American Ethnology*
(Bulletin 61), page 252, Smithsonian
Institution, Washington, DC, 1918.

Minnesota tipis.
—*Courtesy of the Paul and Theresa Harbaugh Collection.*

Noted southern Cheyenne leader Wolf-Chief sits before a tipi with his wife and smokes a pipe. His personal medicines are in the rawhide bag tied over the doorway in this 1890s scene taken in Oklahoma.

—*Photograph by George Bird Grinnell.*

# Sioux Council Songs

Council Songs were sung when the chiefs met in the council tent to decide matters of tribal importance. This tent was placed inside the camp circle and was decorated in various ways.

The first song of this group (gathering at Bull Head, South Dakota, July 4, 1912) was sung by Many Wounds, who preceded the singing by an announcement of the song, which was … translated as follows:

"Tribe, listen to me. I will sing a song of the dead chiefs. What are you saying? The chiefs have come to an end, and I sing their songs. I wish I could do as they have done, but I will try to sing their song.

"Friend—what you are saying is true—the chiefs—are gone—so—I myself will try it."

Frances Densmore, "Teton Sioux Music," *Bulletin of the Bureau of American Ethnology* (Bulletin 61), page 448, Smithsonian Institution, Washington, DC, 1918.

Governor Herreid of South Dakota visiting an Oglalla camp in 1904.

*—Photograph by P. H. Kellogg, Fort Pierre, South Dakota.*
*Courtesy of the Paul and Theresa Harbaugh Collection.*

*Facing page:* Sioux Council tipi taken at Standing Rock Agency, 1884.

*—Photograph by D. F. Barry. Courtesy of the Paul and Theresa Harbaugh Collection.*

1884 Council Tipi, Fort Yates, Dakota Territory.

*—Photograph by D. F. Barry. Courtesy of the Paul and Theresa Harbaugh Collection.*

Hunkpapa Sioux tipi camp on ration day at Standing Rock, Sioux Agency, 1884. Fort Yates is in the background.
—*Photo by Captain (later General) John Pitman. Courtesy of the Paul and Theresa Harbaugh Collection.*

# Death Lodge

Pit'dogede narrates:

When I came home from school at Carlisle, Two Hatchets (a relative) died. A long way from camp his mother put up a tipi for him. She laid him within on the west side, bundled in buffalo robes. She stayed there four nights. There was a big rain. She smoked, puffing the smoke upwards. Big wind. "What do you want?" said a voice. "My son," she said and stretched her arms out towards him, "my son, take care of me!" The dead spoke. "Mother, why do you stay here? I love you. I am watching over you. Give me a smoke." The dead sat up. She fell over. When she came to, the dead man was still sitting up. "Mother, do not stay here. Go home! Lots of people are coming. They might hurt you." She picked up her blanket and ran home. She told the people about it. They went and got the body and buried it. They burned up the tipi.

Elsie Clews Parsons, "Kiowa Tales," *American Folklore Society Memoir* 22. New York, 1929.

Burial tipi, 1885.

*—Photograph by D. F. Barry. Courtesy of the Paul and Theresa Harbaugh Collection.*

# Ghost Lodge

When a son dies the parents cut off some hair from the top of the head with a knife, just above the forehead, placing the hair in a deerskin cover. Then they set up three poles, fastened together at the top and forming a sort of tripod. A cord hung over the top of these holds up the white deerskin pack containing the hair of the deceased. This hair is called the ghost or shade (or wa-na-gi) of the dead person. The deerskin pack hangs horizontally from the poles and the skin is worked with porcupine quills in many lines, and here and there are various kinds of red and blue circular figures sewed on it. All the sod had been cut away from the ground beneath the pack, and on this bare or virgin earth they put a bow and a drinking vessel, each ornamented with porcupine work. Three times a day do they remember the ghost, for whom they put the choicest food in the bowl and water in the drinking vessel. Every article is handled carefully, being exposed to the smoke of sweet-smelling herbs. The pack that is said to contain the ghost is put in the ghost lodge with the knife that he used during life.

The Indians always have observed the custom of smoking pipes and eating while sitting in the ghost lodge. At the back of the lodge they prepare a seat and in the middle they set up two poles similar to these erected outside the entrance to the tents. Before they eat in the lodge, they sacrifice part of the food. Whenever they move the camp or single tent from one place to another, all these sacred objects are packed and carried on a horse kept for this special purpose. This horse has his tail and mane cut off short ... and must mourn as long as the ghost remains unburied; but as soon as the hair is removed from the pack and buried, the horse's hair is allowed to grow long again. As soon as the people stop to encamp, the ghost lodge is set up before any of the others. The articles that are kept there remain for a specified time, perhaps for several years, during which period certain ceremonies are performed. At the end of the allotted time comes the ghost feast, when the ghost pack is opened and the ghost taken out and buried. Then all the people assemble, setting up their tents near the ghost lodge.

J. Owen Dorsey, "A Study of Siouan Cults," *Eleventh Annual Report of the Bureau of American Ethnology*, page 487, Smithsonian Institution, Washington, DC, 1890.

At Pine Ridge in a group with pipe and drum, 1891.

*—Photograph by Morledge. Courtesy of the
Paul and Theresa Harbaugh Collection.*

# Wahpeton Sioux

From the journals of William H. Keating, with the Major Stephen H. Long party in 1823:

They belonged, as we were told, to the Wahkpatoan (Wahpeton), one of the tribes of the Dacotas ... As we rode towards their lodges, we were met by a large party of squaws and children, who formed a very motley group ... The village, to which they directed us, consisted of 30 skin lodges, situated on a fine meadow on the bank of the lake. Their permanent residence ... is on a rocky island in the lake, nearly opposite to, and within a quarter of a mile of, their present encampment. Upon the island they cultivate their cornfields, secure against the aggressions of their enemies. They had been lately engaged in hunting buffalo, apparently with much success. The principal man led us to his lodge, wherein a number of the influential men were admitted, the women being excluded; but we observed that they, with the children, went about the lodge, peeping through all the crevices, and not infrequently raising the skins to observe our motion. They soon brought in a couple of large wooden dishes, filled with pounded buffalo meat, boiled and covered with the marrow of the same animal; of this we partook with great delight.

Later in the day the party returned to these lodges where the chief and his principal men were in waiting. We entered the skin lodge and were seated on fine buffalo robes, spread all round; on the fire, which was in the centre of the lodge, two large iron kettles, filled with choicest pieces of buffalo, were placed ... Our hosts were gratified and flattered at the quantity that we ate; the residue of the feast was sent to our soldiers. In this, and in every other instance where we have been invited to a feast by Indians, we observed that they never eat with their guests.

Hunting lodge of Hunkpapa Sioux, taken near Fort Abraham Lincoln, Dakota Territory, 1884.

*—Photograph by Captain John Pitman.*
*Courtesy of the Paul and Theresa*
*Harbaugh Collection.*

Pine Ridge tipi and log cabin with a sod roof, 1891.

*—Photograph by Morledge. Courtesy of the Paul and Theresa Harbaugh Collection.*

Hostile camp, Pine Ridge, 1891.

—*Photograph by Morledge. Courtesy of the Paul and Theresa Harbaugh Collection.*

# Sioux Boyhood

It is a wonder that any children grew up through all the exposures and hardships that we suffered in those days! The frail tipi pitched anywhere, in the winter as well as in the summer, was all the protection that we had against cold and storms. I can recall times when we were snowed in and it was very difficult to get fuel. We were once three days without much fire and all of this time it stormed violently. There seemed to be no special anxiety on the part of our people; they rather looked upon all this as a matter of course, knowing that the storm would cease when the time came.

I was not more than five or six years old when the (traditional) Indian soldiers came one day and destroyed our large buffalo-skin tipi. It was charged that my uncle had hunted alone a large herd of buffaloes. This was not exactly true. He had unfortunately frightened a large herd while shooting a deer in the edge of the woods.

However, it was customary to punish such acts severely, even though the offense was accidental.

The month of September recalls to every Indian's mind the season of the fall hunt. I remember one such expedition that is typical of many. Our party appeared on the northwestern side of Turtle Mountain, for we had been hunting buffaloes all summer, in the region of the Mouse River, between that mountain and the upper Missouri.

As our cone-shaped tipis rose in clusters along the outskirts of the heavy forest that clothes the sloping side of the mountain, the scene below was gratifying to a savage eye. The rolling yellow plains were checkered with herds of buffaloes. Along the banks of the streams that ran down from the mountains were also many elk, which usually appear at morning and evening, and disappear into the forest during the warmer part of the day. Deer, too, were plentiful, and the brooks were alive with trout. Here and there streams were dammed by the industrious beaver.

The legend-teller, old Smoky Day, was chosen herald of the camp, and it was he who made the announcements. After supper was ended, we heard his powerful voice resound among the tipis in the forest. He would then name a man to kindle the bonfire the next morning. His suit of fringed buckskin set off his splendid physique to advantage.

Charles Alexander Eastman, *Indian Boyhood*, New York, McClure, 1902.

# Mothers and Daughters

One day this careful mother has completed a beautiful little tipi of the skins of a buffalo calf, worked with red porcupine quills in a row of rings jut below the smoke-flaps and on each side of the front opening. In the center of each ring is a tassel of red and white horsehair. The tip of each smoke-flap is decorated with the same material, and the door flap also.

Within there are neatly arranged rawhide boxes for housekeeping, and square bags of soft buckskin adorned with blue and white beads. On either side of the fireplace are spread the tanned skins of a buffalo calf and a deer; but there is no bear, wolf, or wildcat skin, for on these the foot of a woman must never tread! They are for men, and symbolical of manly virtues. There are dolls of all sizes, and a play travois leans against the white wall of the miniature lodge. Even the pet pup is called in to complete the fanciful home of the little woman.

"Now, my daughter," says the mother, "you must keep your lodge in order."

Here the little woman is allowed to invite other little women, her playmates. This is where the grandmothers hold sway, chaperoning their young charges, who must never be long out of their sight. The little visitors bring their workbags of various skins, artistically made and trimmed. These contain moccasins and other garments for their dolls, with which they love to occupy themselves.

The brightly painted rawhide boxes are reserved for food, and in these the girls bring various prepared meats and other delicacies. This is perhaps the most agreeable part of the play to the chaperon, who is treated as an honored guest at the feast!

Charles Alexander Eastman, *Old Indian Days*, New York, McClure, 1907.

A Cheyenne girl dressed in the traditional style of her people carries a puppy as if it were a baby.

# Omaha Lodge

Looking into a lodge and seeing all the inmates sitting or lying on the ground, it would hardly occur to one unfamiliar with Indian life that the ground space of a lodge was almost as distinctly marked off as the different rooms in our composite dwellings; yet such was the fact. The father occupied the middle of the space to the left of the fire as one entered. The mother kept all her household belongings on the left, between the father's place and the entrance. It was thus easy for her to slip in and out of the lodge without disturbing any of the inmates when attending to the cooking and getting the wood and water. If there were young men in the family, they generally occupied the space near the door to the right, where they were in a position to protect the family should any danger arise. If there were old people, their place was on the right, opposite the father. The young girls were farther along, more toward the back part. The little ones clung about the mother but were welcome everywhere and seldom made trouble. Each member had his packs, in which his fine garments and small personal treasures were kept. These packs were set against the wall back of the place belonging to the owner.

Alice C. Fletcher and Francis La Flesche, "The Omaha Tribe," *Twenty-seventh Annual Report of the Bureau of American Ethnology*, page 337, Smithsonian Institution, Washington, DC, 1905–1906.

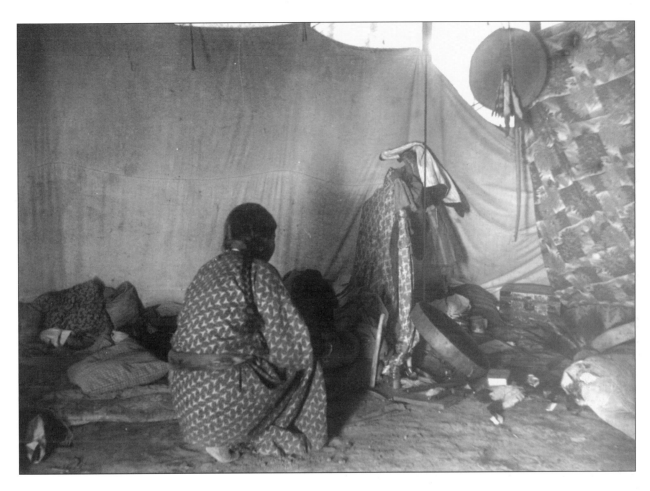

In a Crow tipi a woman is kneeling by her bed; toward the men's side of the lodge are some of the things used by her husband. Hanging highest are his shield and bow and quiver; below lays his drum along with his pipe and a tobacco cutting board. —*Early flash photograph by Miller, posed by Sharp.*

The tipi cover being pulled shut. Though Crow women generally wore their shawls and blankets over their shoulders, for hard work like this they sometimes wrapped them around their waists instead, a style more commonly followed by the men.

Setting up a white canvas lodge on the Crow reservation, circa 1910. The basic frame of poles is already in place, with a ladder in front waiting for someone to climb up and pin the two sides together with carved sticks. One person is putting the tip of a pole through an ear hole.

# Migrations of the Omaha

Written in 1820 by the deputy agent of the Omahas, John Dougherty.

The inhabitants occupy their villages not longer than five months in the year. (Their permanent village was then located on the banks of Omaha Creek near the Missouri River in present-day Dakota County, Nebraska.) In April they arrive from their hunting excursions (with tipis and horses), and in the month of May they attend to their horticultural interests and plant maize, beans, pumpkins, and watermelons … [and] dress the bison skins that have been procured during the winter hunt for the traders who generally appear for the purpose of obtaining them. About June, after having closed the entrances to their several habitations by placing a considerable quantity of brushwood before them, the whole nation departs from the village. At that time they go on their summer buffalo hunt, bringing along their tipis, which are often fancifully ornamented on the exterior with figures in blue and red paint, rudely executed, though sometimes depicted with no small degree of taste … On the return of the nation, which is generally early in September … property buried in the earth is … taken up and arranged in the lodges, which are cleaned out and put in order. The weeds, which during their absence had grown up in every direction through the village, are cut down and removed. A sufficient quantity of sweet corn is next to be prepared for present and future usage.

By the end of October the people were again ready to go on a hunting excursion with their tipis, taking along their newly tanned robes in order to do some trading on the way. This hunt continues until towards the close of December, and during the rigors of the season they experience an alternation of abundance and scarcity of food. After the trading and meat-hunting expedition was finished, they returned to the village to procure a supply of maize from their places of concealment, after which they continue their journey in pursuit of the bison … This bison hunt, from which they brought back quantities of hides and dried meat, was completed in April—time again for planting.

This cabinet card from the 1880s shows a large Crow tipi camp spread across the plains along the Bighorn River, near Crow Agency, back when buffalo hunting and horse raiding were still part of the tribe's daily life. Notice how much smaller the tipis and their poles were back in those nomadic days compared to the fine lodges seen at the Crow tribal fairs of today.    —*Photograph by E. A. Beadle.*

Famous Custer scout Goes Ahead (Crow) is seen by the fire of his lodge. He is camped for the Last Great Gathering of Chiefs, along the Little Bighorn River, in 1909. —*Photograph by Rodman Wannamaker.*

*Facing page:* This Crow lodge has been set up, with the front left wide open for a special event. A well-dressed rider passes by in the foreground.

Irene Not Afraid is an example of a well-dressed and mounted woman of the Crow tribe, circa 1920. Her wool dress is decorated with elk teeth; ahead and behind her are parts of her traditional high-backed saddle. The horse is decked out in beadwork with war symbols painted on his body, probably by her husband or father. —*Photograph by Miller.*

As with most other tribes of the plains, tipi life among the Crow people was full of complex social customs and traditional ceremonials. This scene shows a group of young Crow women being escorted to a special lodge by an elder wrapped in a blanket and wearing a scarf on his head. He was probably praying for them, perhaps also singing honoring songs meant to inform the camp and inspire the women. The tipi next to them has a nicely designed rawhide door; the one in the corner way back is painted all over.

—*Photograph by Rodman Wannamaker.*

On their way to the Last Great Council of Chiefs, several of the Crow leaders are walking through the intertribal camp along the Little Bighorn River to attend the council lodge in 1909.

*—Photograph by Rodman Wannamaker.*

*Above:* Crow Agency Indian fair.

—*Photograph by Strum. Courtesy of the Paul and Theresa Harbaugh Collection.*

*Right:* A woman and her daughter are seen at the edge of a large Crow tipi camp, riding their well-decorated horses. Taken in eastern Montana, circa 1910.

Amid his finery, this elderly man posed with his pipe at the back of his lodge, circa 1915. He is wearing an eagle feather headdress decorated with weasel skins and ribbons. His style of dress was typical of the Crow for the summertime.

# Plains Cree Tipi

The only dwelling was the hide-covered tipi, constructed on a three-pole foundation. In setting up the tipi, three poles were laid on the ground and lashed together with what Wissler calls the "Cheyenne and Arapahoe tie." The poles were raised and the legs of the tripod extended. The rawhide line, which tied the poles, hung down and was staked to the ground inside the tipi. Upon this base 13 poles were laid in counterclockwise order. The total number of poles in the tipi frame varied with the size of the structure.

The cover was hoisted by being lashed to the last pole to be placed in position. It was drawn around the frame and pinned together between the door poles with peeled wooden pegs. Thongs were lashed across the door poles at a height of about five and seven feet to make footrests for fastening the upper part of the cover …

After the cover had been pinned together, the women went inside and shoved the tipi poles out until the cover was taut. The bottom of the cover was fastened to the ground by driving short wooden pegs through eyelets in the cover itself, or through looped thongs fastened to it …

Twelve to twenty buffalo hides were used for a cover. An old woman skilled in cutting covers measured the hides and cut them to the proper shape. Then a feast was prepared and all the women of the camp were invited to partake. After they had eaten, they were assigned to sew at various places on the cover. A bone awl was used to punch holes through which sinew thread was drawn …

Women made the tipi, set it up, owned it. Therefore, a man had to get his wife's consent to have a picture of his spirit helper drawn on the tipi cover.

A back wall of buffalo hide, similar to that used by the Blackfoot, lined the sides of the tipi. Hay was stuffed between this screen and the tipi cover, providing insulation in winter and preventing draughts. In summer the bottom of the cover was rolled up on the poles to a height of about two feet from the ground.

A house form used only for certain dances is the "sapohtowan," … long tipi. Two tripods, made of poles forked at the top, were set up about 25 feet apart. The poles of each tripod were fastened together by interlocking the forks and not by lashing as in an ordinary tipi foundation. A ridgepole laid on the tripods was further supported in the middle by a pair of forked poles interlocked at the point where they joined the ridgepole. Two or three pairs of supports may be used. Ordinary tipi poles were laid against the ridgepole and in a semicircle around the two tripods. Tipi covers or brush were placed over the lower part of the frame, while the upper portion remained open. A fire was built beneath the apex of each tripod.

Joined-together-tipi … was a tipi framework so large that two covers were needed to enclose it. No doorway was made; entrance was obtained by lifting the cover. For the Smoking Tipi Ceremony … four foundation poles were fastened together by interlocking their forked tops and binding them with thongs. Additional poles were laid and two tipi covers drawn over the framework.

While the common tipi was erected by women, these ceremonial structures were set up by men.

David G. Mandelbaum, "The Plains Cree," *Anthropological Papers of the American Museum of Natural History*, Vol. 37, New York, 1940.

Cheyenne women pitching a tipi in 1876.

—*Photograph by S. J. Morrow, Yankton, Dakota Territory. Courtesy of the Paul and Theresa Harbaugh Collection.*

A rustic Yakima tipi with skimpy poles stands next to a ceremonial long lodge made with sticks, poles, and several tipi covers, circa 1920. One man is bringing in an armload of firewood, while another is handling a saddle. Singing, praying, and feasting would have been the main events inside the lodge. The lodge was kept up only for the ceremonial period and not used for actual living.

# Household Furnishings

Beds were made of bundles of dried grass or rushes over which a buffalo robe was thrown. During warm weather the robe alone sufficed. Pillows were rectangular sacks of rawhide filled with duck feathers.

Backrests of peeled willow sticks were used by men of prestige only … suspended from a tripod or from a four-pole base.

Spoons were made from the horns of yearling buffalo … Mussel shells were also much used as spoons. Other spoons and ladles were roughly hewn of wood.

Rawhide bags were utilized for storing food. They were usually made of a single piece of rawhide, doubled over, and sewn along two sides …

Clothes, ornaments, and sometimes food were kept in drawstring bags of tanned hide … Often a rectangle of deer leg skins, untanned, with the dewclaws attached, was sewn on both faces of the bag. The skin from the head of the moose might be used in the same way.

A buffalo paunch was utilized as a water container. When it was filled, a small stick was passed through perforations near the edge of the aperture to close it.

Birch bark containers were used for berries, roots, and even as water buckets. They were of the truncated pyramidal type … the walls rising from a rectangular bottom to an oval opening. A willow hoop was fastened around the inside of the rim … All bark was sewn with split spruce root and was sometimes ornamented with quillwork.

Snow scoops were carved out of split logs. They were made in a single piece and had a straight handle that widened into a rounded blade. They were some four feet long and were about six inches wide at the edge of the blade.

Men kindled the fires, but it was women's work to tend them and collect firewood. Branches for firewood were pulled down and broken off with rawhide thongs … Over the campfire a tripod about five feet high was erected, on which meat was laid to dry and from which cooking utensils were hung. Buffalo chips were much utilized as fuel. On wet days a buffalo skull was smeared with grease and set afire. The skull kept an even heat for a long time.

*Source, facing page:*
David G. Mandelbaum,
"The Plains Cree,"
*Anthropological Papers of
the American Museum of
Natural History*, Vol. 37,
New York, 1940.

A traditional family shows off their home and prized possessions in a painted lodge, circa 1935. The Stoneys are Canadian cousins of the Assiniboine, some of their men long noted for hunting and mountain-climbing skills.

In this tipi camp of the buffalo era on the plains, meat is drying in big slabs on the rack behind the men wearing blankets.

A rustic tipi camp, circa 1910, in northern Alberta, a remote area where traditional lifestyles are still practiced by many Dene families.

Tipis, tents, and a log cabin make up this nature-oriented Dene camp in the northern Canadian wilderness, circa 1920.

A group of Dene traveling by canoe to trade at Fort Rae in northern Canada has stopped to camp along the shore of Great Slave Lake, circa 1920s.

This Dene lodge is surely one of the most rustic examples of a tipi ever photographed, seen in northern Alberta, circa 1890. It has a basic framework of many poles, covered by pieces of canvas, wooden boards, and a variety of other materials. —*Photograph by C. W. Mathers.*

"A family of Eastern Dene (Sarcee) in Native costume." Canada's remote northern wilderness is the traditional home of the Dene people, but various groups of them migrated southward over time. Two of these became the Navajo and Apache of the American Southwest, while another joined the powerful Blackfoot Confederacy and became the Sarcee of the northern plains. The family in this scene was camped on the Sarcee Reserve in the Rocky Mountain foothills near Calgary, circa 1890.

*—Photograph by C. W. Mathers.*

This elder Sarcee woman was preparing a feast of traditional foods over an open fire outside of her lodge in the foothills of southern Alberta, circa 1900. Various cuts of meat, organs, and stuffed pieces of intestine hang from the wooden tripod for smoking and slow cooking, and berries are spread on a ground cloth for drying. She packs pemmican into small sacks. Women spent part of every day sitting like this by their fires, both legs over to one side, whether cooking outside or in their tipis.

—*Photograph by Edward S. Curtis.*

# Buffalo Tongues

Visit to a Blackfoot camp near present-day Calgary, in 1754 by Anthony Hendry, from *Journal of Anthony Hendry 1754–1755.*

Came to 200 tents of Archithinue Natives (Black-feet), pitched in two rows, and an opening in the middle where we were conducted to the leader's tent, which was at one end large enough to contain 50 persons, where he received us seated on a clear (white) buffalo skin, attended by 20 elderly men. He made signs for me to sit down on his right hand: which I did. Our leader lit several grand-pipes, and smoked all round, according to their usual custom; not a word was yet spoke on either side. Smoking being over, buffalo flesh boiled was served round in baskets of a species of bent, and I was presented with 10 buffalo tongues.

David I. Bushnell, Jr., "Villages of the Algonquin, Siouan, and Caddoan Tribes West of the Mississippi," *Bulletin of the Bureau of American Ethnology* (Bulletin 77), page 25, Smithsonian Institution, Washington, DC, 1922.

Blackfoot Lodge.

*—Photograph by Glacier Studio. Courtesy of the Paul and Theresa Harbaugh Collection.*

# Blackfoot Camp

A Blackfoot tipi camp visited and painted in the summer of 1833, reported by Maximilian, Prince of Wied, in *Travels in the Interior of North America*, London, 1843.

The leather tents of the Blackfeet, their internal arrangement, and the manner of loading their dogs and horses, agree, in every respect, with those of the Sioux and Assiniboines, and all the wandering tribes of hunters of the upper Missouri. The tents, made of tanned buffalo skin, last only for one year; they are, at first, neat and white, afterwards brownish, and at the top, where the smoke issues, black, and, at last, transparent, like parchment, and very light inside.

Painted tents, adorned with figures, are very seldom seen, and only a few chiefs possess them. When these tents are taken down, they leave a circle of sod, exactly as in the dwellings of the Esquimaux …

Near the tents they keep their dog sledges, with which they form conical piles resembling the tents themselves, but different from them in not being covered with leather. On these they hang their shields, traveling bags, saddles and bridles; and at some height, out of the reach of the hungry dogs, they hang the meat, which is cut into long strips, their skins, etc. The medicine bag or bundle, the conjuring apparatus, is often hung and fastened to a separate pole, or over the door of the tent. Their household goods consist of buffalo robes and blankets, many kinds of painted parchment bags … wooden dishes (and) large spoons made of the horn of the mountain sheep … In the center of the tent there is a small fire in a circle composed of stones, over which the kettle for cooking is suspended.

David I. Bushnell, Jr., "Villages of the Algonquin, Siouan, and Caddoan Tribes West of the Mississippi," *Bulletin of the Bureau of American Ethnology* (Bulletin 77), page 28, Smithsonian Institution, Washington, DC, 1922.

Ready for the parade. Part of a tipi camp in the Rocky Mountains is seen behind this well-dressed mother and daughter, ready for a tribal parade in their best dresses, on well decorated horses. The mother has a bead-decorated cradleboard hanging from her saddle. The weather must have been hot, as the tipi at left has its cover rolled way up.

# Iron Shirt Gives a Feast

In the lodge of a Blackfoot chief in 1833, reported by Maximilian, Prince of Wied, *Travels in the Interior of North America,* London, 1843.

We were invited on the following day ... to a feast given by the Blackfoot chief Mehkskehme-Sukahs (The Iron Shirt). We proceeded to a large circle in the middle of the camp, enclosed with a kind of fence of boughs of trees, which contained part of the tents and was designed to confine the horses during the night, for the Indians are so addicted to horse stealing that they do not trust each other. The hut of the chief was spacious; we had never before seen so handsome a one; it was a full 15 paces in diameter (40 to 50 feet) and was very clean and tastefully decorated. We took our seats, without ceremony, on buffalo skins, spread out on the left hand of the chief, round the fire, in the centre of the tent, which was enclosed in a circle of stones, and a dead silence prevailed. Our host was a tall, robust man, who at this time had no other clothes than his breechcloth; neither women nor children were visible. A tin dish was set before us, which contained dry grated meat mixed with sweet berries, which we ate with our fingers and found very palatable. After we had finished, the chief ate what was left in the dish.

David I. Bushnell, Jr., "Villages of the Algonquin, Siouan, and Caddoan Tribes West of the Mississippi," *Bulletin of the Bureau of American Ethnology* (Bulletin 77), page 29, Smithsonian Institution, Washington, DC, 1922.

"Indian Fire Dance," reads a note on this brown and white postcard from the 1920s. Although the scene was obviously staged, perhaps for a movie, it does give some idea of how life looked back in the buffalo days, when one of the tribal warrior societies held its public dance by a nighttime fire.

This autumn powwow camp had gathered in 1970 on a meadow at the western end of the Stoney Reserve, located between the city of Calgary, Alberta, and the mountain wilderness of Banff National Park. Stoney hunters are noted for their mountain skills, as symbolized by the drawings on the tipi at left, which include a mountain sheep.

*—Photograph by Adolf Hungrywolf.*

# Notes from a Blackfoot Tipi Camp

When the sun was setting, I walked through the camps of the Lone Eaters and Don't Laugh bands along the shore of the lake. The picturesque lodges, with their painted decorations and blue smoke rising from their tops, were perfectly reflected on the surface of the quiet lake. I crossed a rich meadow, very beautiful in the soft evening light, with its long waving grass and brilliant wild-flowers, and climbed to the summit of a neighboring butte, where I had an excellent view of the entire encampment. On all sides larks, thrushes, and savannah sparrows were singing. In the surrounding meadows, large herds of horses were quietly feeding, while upon the summit of a ridge was a solitary horseman, who had left the noisy camp for quiet and meditation …

Later in the deepening twilight the great cluster of Indian lodges showed a ghostly white against the darkening blue of the eastern sky. When the tipis were lighted by bright inside fires, the circular encampment looked like an enormous group of colored Japanese lanterns, and the flickering lights of the many outside fires resembled fireflies in the summer's dusk.

When I descended from the butte, and again entered the camp circle, twilight had faded into darkness. The bright inside fires revealed upon the canvas of the tipis their weird decorations and the moving shadows of those within. But I soon became confused in my wanderings and lost my way. In the darkness, the tipis all looked alike. There were no streets nor paths, nor any landmarks on the plains, by which I could identify my lodge …

Wolf-Chief came from his lodge to announce that he was giving a feast. He invited guests by shouting each of their names several times in succession …

In another tipi I heard a woman singing softly. Looking within I saw a little hammock, ingeniously made by folding a blanket over two buckskin thongs, swinging from the poles. The baby slept, while its old grandmother gently rocked the hammock, singing a lullaby …

When I finally lay down upon my blanket-bed, it was not to sleep. All in our lodge were disturbed by the many different sounds and even little Tears-In-Her-Eyes was restless in her hammock cradle. There were numberless dogs throughout the camp, fighting and barking. Some were on foraging expeditions, sneaking silently into the lodges in search of food. Menake saw a thieving dog in the act of making away with a side of bacon from our lodge. She made such an outcry that he fled through the doorway with frightened yelps.

Although it was late at night, two small boys, the sons of Running Fisher and Long-Time-Sleeping, came to our lodge and sang a night song as a serenade. According to the Blackfoot custom, it was expected from me to go outside and give them food.

Such incidents in the daily life of an Indian camp (in the 1890s) are like the human experiences we constantly find in the compact cities of civilization. Though the striking extremes of wealth and poverty are absent, the lights and shadows of domestic joy and sorrow, of health and sickness, of pathos and humor, of the grave and the gay, of love and hate, of the old man's wisdom and thoughtfulness and the young man's folly and recklessness—all of these are present in an Indian camp, with even sharper and more impressive contrasts, because of the close association of the people.

Walter McClintock, *The Old North Trail—Life, Legends and Religion of the Blackfeet Indians*, London, Macmillan, 1910.

The tent used during Wolf-Chief's hunt.

"Assiniboine camp on Bow River." Stoneys are the western-most branch of Assiniboines, having moved to the Rocky Mountains in the 1700s and 1800s. This camp was near Banff National Park, circa 1900.

—*Photograph by Edward S. Curtis.*

Here is evidence that tipis continue to be adapted to modern life, as this lodge combines the ancient materials of poles and bark with a few more modern items, as seen in back of a comfortable Stoney family house near Morley, Alberta, in 1978.

—*Photograph by Adolf Hungrywolf.*

# Northwest

The "ecumenical conference" was an annual spiritual encampment during the 1970s that was sponsored by the Stoney tribe. Held on a grassy bluff overlooking the Bow River, it had the spectacular mountains of Banff National Park looming behind, while a herd of semi-wild buffalo roamed a large fenced paddock in the other direction. Spiritual leaders and practitioners came from all over North America to share tribal traditions as well as teachings from the Bible. They brought some of the tipis in this scene; the Stoneys put others up for their guests. The two "pole lodges" in the foreground are of an ancient style, made with a circle of slim tipi poles covered with moss. Many participants slept in their trailers and vehicles; others joined a tent village spread out in the woods near the cookhouse and conference area, off to the right.

# Conical Mat Lodge

# Salish Conical Lodge

The conical lodge, or tent of poles covered with mats made of sewed tules, was the common family house of the Coeur d'Alene, summer and winter. In summer the lodge was pitched on the surface of the leveled ground. Generally single layers of mats were used. In winter it was pitched over an excavation, a few inches to a foot and a half in depth, and the excavated earth banked up around the base. Dry grass, dry pine needles, or pieces of bark were placed around the bottom of the mats to prevent decay. Double and treble layers of mats were used in the wintertime. These lodges varied in diameter from about five to upward of ten meters. It seems that the foundation was almost always made of three poles. I did not hear of any particular method of tying the poles. In all particulars these lodges appear to have been the same as the common mat tent used by the Thompson and all interior Salish tribes. From one to three related families occupied a lodge. Many were occupied by single families.

All the tribes used summer lodges made of tule mats laid on a framework of poles. These lodges were of two main types—circular and oblong. The circular mat tent was the most common and was looked upon as the family house. As a rule, they were not very large, and the poles were arranged on a three-pole foundation. They were also used a great deal in the wintertime, when they were covered with from two to four layers of mats instead of one, as in the summer. They were usually occupied by one or two families, and when well covered were warm and quite snow and rain proof.

James A. Teit, "The Salishan Tribes of the Western Plateaus," *Forty-fifth Annual Report of the Bureau of American Ethnology*, Smithsonian Institution, Washington, DC, 1927.

# Expanding Tipi Life

It seems that very long ago no skin lodges of any kind were used; but some of the Flathead, and possibly also Pend d'Oreilles, are said to have used a few made of buffalo and elk hide, as far back as tradition goes. After buffalo hunting was engaged in by the Coeur d'Alene, tents of buffalo skins like those used by the Flathead and neighboring Plains tribes began to supersede all other kinds of lodges, and soon became the only kind used in traveling. When buffalo skins became scarce, light canvas tents were substituted for the skin tents. At the present day (1920s), these and white men's tents are altogether used in camping. Some of the buffalo-skin tents were ornamented with painted designs.

James A. Teit, "The Salishan Tribes of the Western Plateaus," *Forty-fifth Annual Report of the Bureau of American Ethnology*, Smithsonian Institution, Washington, DC, 1927.

# Brush Lodge

Temporary brush lodges of poles and branches of coniferous trees, chiefly fir and balsam, were used by hunting parties and by people traveling in the mountains. Most of them were slightly oblong, almost like the bark lodges. A few were conical. On hunting grounds where good bark abounded, bark lodges were always used as hunting lodges.

# Women's Lodge

Women's lodges, used by women during their isolation periods, and lodges of adolescent maidens, were chiefly small tents or conical lodges placed at some distance from other dwellings and covered with mats, bark, brush, or old skins. Sometimes in the summer women used a mere shelter or shade of mats or bark.

James A. Teit, "The Salishan Tribes of the Western Plateaus," *Forty-fifth Annual Report of the Bureau of American Ethnology*, Smithsonian Institution, Washington, DC, 1927.

# Long Lodge

The long communal lodge was also used, especially at gatherings and at summer resorts, where many people congregated temporarily. In fair weather the long lodge used was often a single, one-sided lean-to, with the fires built in the open along the front. Sometimes windbreaks of mats or of brush were extended across one or both ends. If the lodge was to be used for a number of weeks, or if the weather was cold, and there was a good supply of mats on hand, another similar lean-to was built facing the first, and the spaces at the ends between the two were filled in, thus making a double lean-to lodge. An exit or doorway was left at each end. The long opening at the top was quite wide and served as an outlet for the smoke. Sometimes, if people were camped in a single lean-to and cold, windy weather came on, half of the single lean-to was taken down and pitched opposite the other half, and a double lean-to thus made. However in warm summer weather the airy single lean-to seems to have been the customary type where there was a large crowd. Usually single lean-tos were in a straight line, but sometimes they extended more or less in an arc or half-moon shape. This depended on the length of the lodge and the nature of the ground. Some of them ranged in length from 30 to 50 meters. The construction of these as well as of the double lean-to was the same as among the Thompson, Nez Perce, and neighboring tribes. Construction varied sometimes in details ... Some double lean-tos ... accommodated as many people as could lie in them from end to end on both sides—from 75 to 100 or more. The people inhabiting them lived at other times (or when at home) in mat tents and other family lodges.

A large, permanent long lodge of the double lean-to type, constructed with great care, was erected at all the principal villages as a gathering place or general meeting house for the people of the village and as a winter dance house. It was also used for the accommodation of visitors. When not otherwise in use, it served as headquarters for young men engaged in training during the wintertime and was inhabited by them. During most winter nights, singing and dancing could be heard in this lodge; and at frequent intervals most of the people congregated there, especially evenings, to see the young men practicing their songs and medicine dances or playing games.

*Source, previous page:* James A. Teit, "The Salishan Tribes of the Western Plateaus," *Forty-fifth Annual Report of the Bureau of American Ethnology,* Smithsonian Institution, Washington, DC, 1927.

Nez Perce—"Chief Joseph's camp, showing part of circle," states a note on the back of this print, circa 1910. The camp looks like it was intended to be there for a while, with meat drying racks set up, a big barn, and a corral out behind. Blankets and clothes are being aired out by many of the lodges, possibly after a rainstorm or perhaps a very exciting and hot dance. The nearest tipi may have been used for a big gathering, as its cover has been left partly open in front, with a sheet of canvas draped over the tie strings. Riding gear and other household items are piled out front, covered by a tarp.

# Lodge Furnishings

House furnishings, as among other interior tribes, were very simple. The parts of the lodge where people sat and slept were covered with "bed" or "floor" mats of rushes. Some other coarser, squarer mats were used to some extent as seats and food was placed on them, preparatory to cooking. Often a layer of dry pine needles, or dry grass, or fine boughs of fir, balsam, hemlock, or cedar, laid regularly, all the butts one way, was spread all over the floor of the lodge. If these materials were scarce they were spread where the people slept and the bed mats were laid on top. No stools or benches were used. Often blocks of wood, pieces of tree trunks or large branches, and slabs of bark were used as seats at open fires outside of lodges in the mountains or in the woods. No special backrests were made. People lounged on the beds, using as backrests the rolled-up bedding, rolls of skins, bundles of any kind, full bags, or large stiff baskets placed mouth down.

Sometimes short pieces of plank, or slabs of stiff bark placed on edge and properly supported, were used as temporary backrests.

Beds were made next to the walls of the lodge. The sleepers had, as a rule, their heads toward the wall and their feet toward the fire. If the lodge was very narrow, beds were made sideways along the fire. Some people preferred this way when there was plenty of room. Beds were made of skins spread over mats and grass or brush, or sometimes of mats alone, or of skins alone spread over these materials. Skins of buffalo, bear, goat, and elk with the hair on were much used as bedding; also skins of deer, sheep, and old robes of any kind. For bed coverings, robes were used; possibly those of buffalo and elk were most common. Pillows generally consisted of bunches of dry grass and pieces of robes, or rolls of matting. Often the head of the bed was simply raised by heaping up grass or brush under the bedding. Sacks of clothes and other soft materials were also used for this purpose. No pillows of bulrush down were used, and very few of hair or feathers. The spaces next to the door of the lodge were used for keeping the cooking utensils and for storage. Some kinds of food stored in sacks and baskets, dressed hide, and many other things were placed out of the way in the spaces between the beds and the base of the lodge walls. As a rule, dressed skins, clothes, valuables, and odds and ends were placed near the head or side of the bed. Some men kept their

Indian family at home in 1909.

    —*Photograph by Martin. Courtesy of the Paul and Theresa Harbaugh Collection.*

medicine bags at the head of the bed or hidden under the pillow. Workbags, quivers, and clothes were hung up near the beds or in convenient places. For this purpose, cords and light poles were often attached to the poles of the lodge. Moccasins were hung on these or put under the foot of the bed. In some lodges small shelves, consisting of racks of light poles, were tied to the poles. Meat and other foods were dried and stored on them. Sometimes a framework for smoking meat and fish and for drying clothing extended across the lodge above the fire. Water, cooking utensils, and the larger tools were kept just inside the door.

Circular baskets were used as kettles for boiling food. Meat and other foods were roasted on sticks before the fire or baked in hot ashes. Small bowls hollowed out of knots of trees and others made of bark and basketry were only occasionally used … Parties on short hunting and traveling trips, having no mats and baskets with them, spread food on twigs and the small ends of branches heaped together. They also did boiling in pouches; but as a rule they roasted meat on sticks, before the fire. They carried no bedding and slept wrapped in their robes on a couch of fir boughs or similar material.

Some small bowls were made of mountain ram's horn. Spoons and ladles were of horn and wood. The largest ones were all of mountain ram's horn. Smaller ones were made of goat horn or buffalo horn. Large and small wooden spoons were used, and most of them were made of balsam poplar wood (*Populus balsamifera*). Spoons made from the skullcaps of deer and possibly those of other animals were fairly common. Tongs and stirrers were made of wood …

Fire was made with the common hand drill … The hearth stick was of poplar, willow, or various other kinds of wood. The top stick was generally made of cedar …

Tinder consisted of very dry cedar bark shredded and teased very fine. It was carried in a bag made for the purpose, and in wet or damp weather was worn underneath the arm close to or within the armpit. In places where cedar bark was scarce, bark of other trees, dry grass, and other materials were used. In permanent camps, fires were banked or otherwise attended to, and never allowed to go out entirely. Fire was carried from one place to another by means of cedar bark slow matches.

James A. Teit, "The Salishan Tribes of the Western Plateaus." *Forty-fifth Annual Report of the Bureau of American Ethnology*, Smithsonian Institution, Washington, DC, 1927.

The stars and stripes fly high over the Flathead tribe's big Fourth of July encampment at Arlee, Montana, circa 1910. The fine white lodges lined up in this scene were only one part of the big tribal circle. Dances, parades, games, and feasts were daily events then, as they still are today at this same location in western Montana.

# THE NORTHERN ROCKIES

# The Flathead Tipi

The miserable short-poled tipi the Flathead never knew. The Flathead contact with the Plains [tribes] was never important in pre-horse days, so that there was no incentive to take over Plains' ways before the bison trek began in earnest, especially poorer ways. But when the horse brought them into intimate contact even with hostile plainsmen, they took over the improved tipi, a tent made almost lordly by the increased length of the lodge poles, which the greater mobility made possible. They made the Plains' pavilion theirs with but one defect. They did not use the side wall for the interior, that drape which not only improved the appearance of the inside but also shut out the draft.

The Salish preferred to cut the lodge poles in the spring, while the sap was still in them, and to season them dry over several weeks, ordinarily procuring new poles each year. Fifteen poles went into an erection of the larger tents, but regardless of the number dictated by the varying sizes of [the] dwellings, the foundation was made of four poles that were most carefully chosen …

The material was bison hide, taken from cows in the spring to save the arduous toil of removing the winter hair. It took from seven to fifteen scraped hides to make one tent, in all creating a load heavy enough to require a separate pack horse on the march. In fact the great thickness and bulk of the bison hide made it desirable for related families to pair off and occupy one tent in common during the winter bison hunt, each being responsible for the transportation of one-half the tent.

The women made and in theory owned the tents. This was most reasonable since there was no mean trick in the designing, cutting, and fitting, and the toil involved was considerable. Except for the bride's first tipi, which she rather ceremonially made by herself, a new tipi cover was made by all the women of the camp who would help. Ordinarily there was no difficulty in persuading six to ten skilful women to help since it was a fine time for gossip, exhibition of skill, and for eating liberal repasts laid out by the hostess. Cover designers were considered experts and were admired by all the village. This woman might direct all the work, although specialists in certain particular skills were usually called in: one for the ticklish job of designing and fitting the smoke hole wings, one for fitting the top, one known for her ability in sewing up the front, and so on. These specialists worked without fee, content with the adulation of the others and the joy of bossing subordinates.

The lodge cover was made in three belts or rings. The lowest ring was not only the easiest to design and make but also the narrowest. While in bulk it was great, covering the greatest circumference of the tent, it was seldom more than two feet broad. But designing the middle layer required skill, for if this were not adeptly done, the tipi would fail to have a symmetrical cone shape. The designer herself supervised the cutting of this piece. Often another designer would take charge of cutting and sewing the top layer that contained the smoke hole. If this were not made properly, the fire would not draw well. The sewing was made with a bone awl. The upper layers were sewn to overlap those under them. Using mere awls, it was necessary to push the sinew in through the holes after the piercing instrument had been withdrawn.

The cover made, the designer directed that it be laid on its poles to see if it would fit. Adjustments were almost always necessary. The places where the poles came were observed, and the seamstresses marked these places so that the falls of the thongs could be sewn on.

The cover was then removed from the poles and the task of inserting the wings for the smoke hole was begun. These controlled the smoke and thereby the comfort of the inhabitants. These were sewn to the upper belt of the cover, and little pockets were inserted in their tips to receive the poles, which would manipulate them from below. If the wind were from directly behind the lodge, the poles would be moved to open both wings. If it were from one side of the lodge, the windward wing would be closed or almost closed. If the wind blew directly onto the front of the lodge, both wings would be closed.

The decoration of the lodge came next; for the most part [it was] the job of the senior male inhabitant. Here were painted in bright colors his war honors or great dreams. More often the men painted each of the three levels a different color. The women practiced but one style of decoration. Often the tails of the bison were not removed when the scraping process took place. When the cover was drawn taut over its poles, these tails would sweep outward in graceful arcs, a ring of tails for each layer of the cover. This was so well thought of that often when it was convenient to remove the tails in the hide-dressing, they were sewn back on.

The tipi was now considered finished and the family gave as sumptuous a feast of dedication as they could afford. When all had eaten well, speeches were made and the family offered the good wishes and prayers of all.

The setting up of a lodge after the day's journey was a task easily accomplished by one woman in about 15 minutes. If the inhabitants were traveling alone or with but a few, the husband selected the lodge site. If a village circle were to be formed, each family or related groups of households had their position in the ring assigned to it by the sub-chief. The lodge poles were laid upon the ground, their upper ends together and their lower ones spread apart about one foot. A rawhide thong was then wrapped around the upper ones some three

to four times, right where the crossing was expected to be, and tied. The subsequent spreading of the poles was relied upon to increase the tension enough to make a firm junction. A stone was then placed against the foot of the pole that was to become the rearmost. Grasping the opposite pole, the woman now raised the four foundation poles together, spreading in the meantime the two mentioned into their approximate final positions. The two others could be expected to rise as well and to spread slightly, enough to keep the whole from falling down while the woman could run to grasp one of the side poles and move it into its approximate position. The fourth pole was now set so that the four foundation poles enclosed a square. These corrected, the woman proceeded to insert in one of the square's faces the two supplementary poles that were to form the door. These were the longest poles of the lodge and were spread wide apart. The rest of the supernumerary poles were then set upon the foundation until the lodge's site has assumed its correct circular form. The last poles to be set were the control poles for the wings that were put into position after the cover had been tied in place. This was done by securing the cover to one of the entrance poles, then encircling all of the poles to arrive at the opposite entrance pole to which that side of the

Noted dancer and singer Sam Findlay (Flathead) is dressed up on horseback for a special celebration at an intertribal tipi camp in the mountains of Glacier National Park, circa 1930. Present were members of the Blackfoot, Kootenay, and Flathead tribes, all of whom camped and traveled in this region for ages before it became a park.

*—Photograph by Ruhles.*

cover was made fast. The wing poles were then inserted into their loops. Next the woman tied all the thongs to their proper poles from the interior. This done, she staked down the lower edge, then fastened up the front with skewers that had been made for the purpose.

The first job in the interior was the preparation of the fireplace directly under the smoke hole. If logs were available, three fair-sized pieces were laid along a square; the face nearest the door was left free so as not to encumber the cook's work. This was done to prevent the sparks from flying onto the inflammable floor covering. The boiling hole was next dug on one side or other of the cook's position. This was lined with hide, the method of boiling being by dropping hot stones into the skin-lined hole.

The floor covering came next. In summer the base flooring was of matting, almost the only weaving technique retained by the Flathead. In winter a warm and springy base was made with fir boughs, if the camp were westerly enough to provide them. Bison robes folded once were then laid upon the floor, the creased edges away from the fireplace. The family's goods were stored in these folds, being pushed far back against the fold and the edge of the lodge to make the bottom draft-proof.

The mats used by the Salish for floor padding were made from two raw materials. They considered those made from cattails the best, being heavier and more durable. These they used when in the more permanent western camps, but because of their heavy pack weight they were too cumbersome to take to the plains. Mats of various long grasses were made to accommodate the winter mobility.

The interior was divided into three triangular segments. The wall side of the rearmost element was primarily used as storage space for food. On each side of this the wall space was used to store horse gear, tools, and weapons. The family slept between the storage space and the fire. When everything was in order, the last to be moved into the lodge was the semi-sacred backrest for the man. It was also the first object to be removed when the tent was struck. This consisted of a tripod supporting a long, curving, flexible triangle of rods from its apex. It held the man's weapons as well as giving him a place to recline, but its sacred character was derived from its being the resting place of his sumesh bundle. While this piece of furniture was considered the man's property, it was made by his wife who had complete responsibility for its care.

*Source, previous page:* Harry Holbert Turney-High, "The Flathead Indians of Montana," *Memoirs of the American Anthropological Association*, No. 48, Menasha, Wisconsin, 1937.

This hand-colored postcard reads: "Indian Ceremonies, Blackfeet Indians, Canadian North-West." Several tipi covers were draped over a lengthy framework of tipi poles and horse travois to make a large shaded arena for an important council meeting. The photo was taken in the 1880s, shortly after the end of the buffalo-hunting and war-raiding days, when many women still made travois to use with their horses.

This snapshot was taken about 1915 in the Rocky Mountains of western Montana during the setting up of a family hunting camp by a group of Flathead-Salish people from around Arlee. A canvas tent is already up on the right, while the new tipi poles at left still require their covering. The man on the wagon wears traditional clothing, which was still common among conservative Flatheads in those days.

# The Flat Pipe Keeper's Lodge

The Flat Pipe keeper's lodge was a large one, undecorated on the outside except for a portion painted red around the door …

The interior of the keeper's lodge was arranged as follows. In the center was the family hearth. About midway between this and the north segment was the square incense hearth, with the west half of black sand and the east of red. At the north, close to the wall, was the Pipe bed and place for the Pipe tripod. The bed … was made of a buffalo robe over sagebrush. At each end was a willow backrest, and over each rest a robe … The Pipe bundle was either laid on the bed close to the wall or else hung on the tripod …

The keeper's sleeping bed, with its backrest toward the north, was a little removed from the Pipe bed, toward the west; the co-keeper's [was] in a corresponding position toward the east. The Pipe child commonly slept on the Pipe bed, alongside of and to the south of the Pipe bundle …

The keeper's lodge, as the depository of the Flat Pipe and the dwelling of the consecrated custodians thereof, had to be treated with great respect. This respect was formalized in a number of ritual and other observances.

No one was permitted to step over the incense hearth, under penalty of being inflicted with fits. Anyone entering the keeper's lodge, or leaving it or passing from one part of it to another, always had to walk clockwise. No one … could throw stones or sticks at the keeper's lodge. Children were not allowed to play or fool or romp around it, but were taught and trained to be quiet around it and to observe reverence toward it. No whistling or crying was permitted in the keeper's lodge … Dogs were never allowed to enter … Breaking bones to extract marrow was prohibited … There was a very strict prohibition against telling lies … Neither the keeper nor others were permitted to tell folktales of the vulgar or obscene … type.

John M. Cooper, "The Gros Ventres of Montana: Part II—Religion and Ritual," *The Catholic University of America Anthropological Series* 16. Washington, DC, 1956.

# Gros Ventres Tipi Life

The lodges of the Gros Ventres were made from buffalo hides, the number used in each depending on the size of the lodge. They were sewn together with sinew. The women selected the poles for the lodge, as well as for the travois, and were responsible for erecting and taking down the lodge, for the arrangement of the interior, for the making of the travois, and for the packing and moving of impediments.

The foundation of three poles for the lodge was tied together and then raised as a unit. The other poles were arranged one by one, starting with those of the front. The cover of buffalo hides was tied to one pole, the "backbone," which was placed at the center-back, the cover then being drawn into place and fastened securely at the front, with small wooden pins usually made of cherry tree wood. The ordinary Gros Ventre lodge stakes were shaped like a pin with a relatively small head. One informant, however, stated that this form of stake often came loose where the cover became taut with the wind, and that she had found the forked type, first observed by her many years ago when visiting another tribe to the south, far more satisfactory.

Old lodge covers were saved and cut up to make a sort of lining at the bottom of the lodge in winter, and the snow scraped away to make place for the lodge was piled up on the outside thereof for extra warmth. In summer the ground inside the lodge was covered with willows, sagebrush, or rye grass. Decorated robes as windbreaks were sometimes suspended in the lodge behind the fancy backrests, which were made by the women from slender willow rods. The women gathered and peeled the rods, although the young men helped straighten them by pulling them through their teeth. A willow ring encircled the fireplace and a broom of buckbrush was always kept handy. Personal belongings were neatly disposed against the wall of the lodge and in front of these were placed the skins that served as bedding by night and as seats by day. The painted parfleches were given prominence to lend colorful touches. Dishes, utensils, and stored food were suspended from poles well off the floor …

A circle camp of tipis sits beside a community of wood homes and barns in the eastern Washington reservation of Colville in the early 1900s. Many riders are heading for the circle, perhaps to parade around it in advance of a big dance to be held inside the sheltered structure at the center.

The place of honor was at the back of the lodge, opposite the door. Here at night slept the "man of the house" and his senior wife, if he were a polygamist; the other wives and children [slept] on either side. Coming Daylight described the arrangement of her father's lodge as it was before she was sent to live with her grandmother. Her father and one wife slept at the rear, the bedding placed parallel to the door; she and her mother had their bedding to the left as one entered the lodge, and perpendicular in regard to the opening, sleeping with their heads to the rear and feet to the door; while her father's unmarried brothers were similarly placed as she and her mother, but on the opposite side of the lodge …

The lodge poles had to be transported separately from the cover. The poles were cut when needed, and a hole was burned about four inches from the top of each. When the lodge was up, the free ends of the short strings of buckskin, run through these holes, fluttered in the breeze, making a fine decoration. The more practical purpose of the holes, however, was to allow a number of poles to be strung together for moving. For water transport, not more than six poles would be so tied together, a strong line running through the holes, leaving a loop to go about the horse's neck. Another line was tied around the six, about in the middle, to hold the poles together as the horse dragged them through the water. A mounted horse could draw two sets of six poles across the river at one time, one set on each side, but could not take all the poles for a lodge on a single trip. Meat packed in skin bags was often lashed to the poles and did not suffer in transit. Occasionally older children rode across the river on these poles, and some people paddled across straddling a single log.

John M. Cooper, "The Gros Ventres of Montana: Part II—Religion and Ritual," *The Catholic University of America Anthropological Series* 16. Washington, DC, 1956.

Dated July 14, 1919, this photo shows part of a circle camp of tipis in the hills of Colville Reservation in eastern Washington. A crowd has gathered within the circle on foot and horseback, surrounding a seated group of drummers and singers. A man to the right of them begins his solitary war dance, while others in dance clothes wait to join him. A rustic dance hall is available in case the weather turns bad, though the tipis would be safer in heavy rain than that partial roof of canvas sheets.

Long before his tribe's name (Yakima) became synonymous with Washington apples, this well-dressed man posed proudly as the head of his family in their opened tipi home, circa 1885.

—*Courtesy of the Click Relander Collection.*

A Yakima home, eastern Washington, circa 1920.  —*Photograph by Lee Moorhouse.*

Yakima tipi and salmon-drying scaffold, circa 1920.     *—Photograph by Lee Moorhouse.*

Plateau—This ceremonial long lodge of poles covered by mats was photographed around 1890 near Pendleton, Oregon.

—*Photograph by M. M. Hazeltine.*

Chief No-Shirt's camp, along the Umatilla River, Oregon. The small tipi in back is of canvas, while the two nearer ones have both canvas and mats, inside and out. The one at left has an interesting method of securing the combined covers, with long thin poles over the outside, tied down by a rope that goes around them.

—*Photograph by Lee Moorhouse.*

# SOUTHWEST

These Jicarilla Apache people were along the southern fringe of tipi-using tribes, sometimes taking theirs down into Mexico. This camp was photographed in New Mexico, circa 1915.

# Chiricahua Apache Life-Ways

The woman not only makes the furnishings of the home but is responsible for the construction, maintenance, and repair of the dwelling itself and for the arrangement of everything it. She provides the grass and brush beds and replaces them when they become too old and dry. With a stiff grass broom or with a leafy branch, she sweeps out the interior, if that is necessary. However, formerly "they had no permanent homes, so they didn't bother with cleaning."

The dome-shaped dwelling or wickiup (was) the usual house type for all the Chiricahua bands … but a "peaked" home of brush, roughly resembling a conical Plains tipi in shape, is also made. Said a Chiricahua informant:

"Both the tipi and the oval-shaped house were used when I was a boy. The oval hut was covered with hide and was the best house. The more well-to-do had this kind. The tipi type was made of brush. It had a place for a fire in the center. It was just thrown together."

Both types were common even before my time. For the girl's puberty rite, the tipi type was used. Ten or more poles are used in the tipi. The number depends on the person who makes it. It is a woman's work to do it, though sometimes the men would help a little.

A few of the eastern Chiricahua had a tipi like that of the Mescalero. Sometimes it was made with a three-pole base and sometimes with a four-pole base. The three-pole base was more common. In my day (late 1800s) it was cloth covered, but the old people talk of them and say that, before the whites and the Spanish were here, hides were used …

The eastern Chiricahua didn't drag the poles of the tipi when they moved. They put them on the front of the saddle, as many as they could carry, and then went back for the rest. Usually they just discarded them though. They could always make new ones.

Morris Edward Opler, *An Apache Life-Way*, The University of Chicago Press, Chicago, Illinois, 1941.

A ceremonial encampment of Jicarilla Apache people and their friends, near Dulce, New Mexico, in 1915. The tipi camp was set up in a circle around the medicine lodge of brush seen at right, similar to Sun Dance camps of northern tipi-using tribes.

An elongated circle camp of tipis at the Apache ceremonial gathering near Dulce, New Mexico, in 1915. The brush-covered medicine lodge arbor is in the distance, with many of the tipis gathered near it.

Part of the Apache ceremonial encampment near Dulce, New Mexico, in 1915.

*Previous page:* Jicarilla Apache warrior and elder Casamaria and his family, standing beside their dual home of canvas tipi and log house covered by adobe mud and a board roof. He and his wife wear traditional clothing, including his leggings and breechcloth; the two granddaughters beside them have on more modern dresses and shoes. Beside them is a pile of fresh melons from the garden, along with a sheet of rawhide covered with drying beans or berries.

*Above:* A more distant view of the Casamaria homestead, showing a second tipi that was perhaps for the family of a son or daughter, or possibly for visitors. Details around the place show this to have been a hard-working and creative family, with a large fenced garden, drying racks and tables, and a good barn and corral with a nice pile of hay. Near Dulce, New Mexico, in 1915.

Jicarilla Apache elder Casamaria again, this time showing how to make old-style arrows on the ground by his tipi in 1915.

Jicarilla Apache men and women are gathered in their finest dress to sing, dance, and parade during their ceremonial encampment in 1915.

Foot racing with sacred symbolism was part of the ceremonial tipi camp among the Jicarilla Apache in 1915. Tipis are in the distant background.

Another scene of the sacred foot races taking place near the tipis of the Jicarilla Apache ceremonial camp in 1915.

# Apache Tipis

Quoting from reports on the expedition of Francisco Vásquez de Coronado, 1540–42, during a visit with the "Querechos," thought to have been Apaches:

They fasten … poles at the top and spread them apart at the bases, then cover this framework with buffalo hides. They load the dogs (larger than those of Mexico) like beasts of burden and make light pack saddles for them like ours, cinching them with leather straps … The dogs go about with sores on their backs like pack animals … When they move—for they have no permanent residence anywhere, since they follow the cattle (buffalo) to obtain food—these dogs transport their houses for them. In addition to what they carry on their backs, they transport the poles for the tents, dragging them fastened to their saddles. A load may be from 30 to 50 pounds, depending on the dog.

Herbert Eugene Bolton, *Coronado, Knight of Pueblos and Plains*, University of New Mexico Press, Albuquerque, 1949.

*Following page:* Titled "In Apache Land," this 1920s hand-colored postcard was distributed by the Fred Harvey Company as part of its Southwest tourist trade, especially along the route of the Santa Fe Railroad. The card has this caption on back:

"The Apache Indians were until recently the most warlike of all the Southwestern Indians and have caused the government of the United States, as well as the early settlers, no end of trouble. Today, with their number fast diminishing, and with several forts on or near their scattered reservations with the railroad as an ally, the government has no trouble with them and the Indian has turned his talents to the weaving of baskets and plaques and is at last enjoying the fruits of his labors at peace."

# Red and White Bell Tents

Quoting Don Juan de Oñate in his report on an expedition of 1599:

There were 50 tents made of tanned hides, very bright red and white in color and bell-shaped, with flaps and openings, and built as skillfully as those of Italy, and so large that in the most ordinary ones, four different mattresses and beds were easily accommodated (it has been estimated that this would require a tipi at least 12 feet in diameter). The tanning is so fine that although it should rain bucketfuls, it will not pass through nor stiffen the hide, but rather, upon drying, it remains as soft and pliable as before ... The Sergeant Mayor bartered for a tent and brought it to this camp, and although it was so very large, it did not weigh over two arrobas (50 pounds).

> Herbert Eugene Bolton, *Spanish Exploration in the Southwest, 1542 to 1706 (Original Narratives of Early American History)*, New York, C. Scribner's Sons, 1916.

A part of the large ceremonial encampment among the Jicarilla Apache near Dulce, New Mexico, in 1915.

# Sweat Lodges

Cheyenne sweat lodges like this could most always be found along the edges of tipi camps, used mainly by men for spiritual and ceremonial reasons. Made with willow sticks tied in the shape of an upside-down basket, then covered with old tipi covers, robes, and quilts, these were often large enough to seat 10 to 15 men. Usually a prescribed number of hot rocks was placed in a pit at the center of this lodge. Some used sage for floor coverings; others used slough grass. Many just sat on the ground. Women also used small lodges for healing and personal purification.

# Salish Sweat Lodges

Sweathouses were of the common dome-shaped type, with a framework of bent willows, such as those used by all the plateau tribes. A hole was dug to one side of the entrance to hold the stones. The covering was of bark or grass, over which was laid sod or earth to the depth of from five to twelve centimeters. Temporary sweathouses had the sticks farther apart, and were covered when in use with robes, skins, or closely woven pliable mats in one or two layers. After the introduction of canvas and woolen blankets, very few earth-covered sweathouses were made, blankets or tents being used as covering whenever required. The floor of the sweathouse was covered with soft brush or with grass. Most of them were small and could accommodate only one or two persons. A very few were made large enough for five or six people.

James A. Teit, "The Salishan Tribes of the Western Plateaus," *Forty-fifth Annual Report of the Bureau of American Ethnology*, Smithsonian Institution, Washington, DC, 1927.

# Ojibwa Sweat Lodges

The Ojibwa villages were supplied with the usual sweathouses, a small frame covered with blankets or other material, so often described. Resembling these were the shelters prepared for the use of certain old men who were believed to possess the power of telling of future events and happenings.

David I. Bushnell, Jr., "Villages of the Algonquin, Siouan, and Caddoan Tribes West of the Mississippi," *Bulletin of the Bureau of American Ethnology* (Bulletin 77), page 16, Smithsonian Institution, Washington, DC, 1922.

*Previous page:* A varied number of willows is used to make a sweat lodge, often 12 or 14, though sometimes up to 100, depending on particular rituals and customs. This Cheyenne sweat lodge included the use of a buffalo skull.

*Above:* Apache—An old man adjusts the covers of a small sweat lodge in which he and his friend at right will sit to purify themselves.

Getting dressed after a sweat bath, as seen among the northern Cheyenne near Lame Deer, Montana, circa 1910. While many tribes end their sweat baths by swimming in cold water, those of the plains often just put their clothes back on afterwards, like these old fellows here. Their lodge is a big one, covered with a canvas tipi, several quilts, and an Oriental rug. This place was used often for sweats, as evidenced by the big pile of old sweat rocks out behind, next to the buffalo skull. Assuming the front of this lodge is facing east, as most do, the sweat was held early in the morning, since the sun still casts fairly long shadows. We can only wonder what powerful old songs these men sang while they sat in the damp heat inside. Presumably one of them will be riding back home on the saddled horse parked nearby.

# PAINTED TIPIS

# Blackfoot Painted Lodges

Of all types of primitive dwellings, the tipi of the Plains tribes, with its conical shape, tapering poles, and ingeniously devised "ears" for facilitating the upward draught for the inside fire, is one of the most picturesque and beautiful. It has been evolved in the distant past to meet the requirements of a nomadic people for shelter. Like the snow igloo of the far distant Esquimaux, it displays much skill in the adaptation of available materials to the necessities of their environment. It is a perfect habitation for comfort, convenience, and good ventilation in both summer and winter. Its design and interior arrangements are so complete, they never change. In recent years canvas has been substituted as a covering in place of buffalo skins, because of the practical extinction of the buffalo.

No one who has seen the "White City" of the Blackfeet, during their annual Festival of the Sun, can ever forget the strange and fascinating beauty of the scene. With the snow-capped Rocky Mountains for a background, hundreds of white tipis, uniform in shape, and pitched in perfect order by clans, are spread upon the plain in a great circular encampment.

The rapidity with which such a great camp can be either "pitched" or "struck" is almost incredible. Catlin, in describing the sudden striking of a similar camp by the Sioux, says: "At the time announced, the lodge of the chief is seen flapping in the wind, a part of the poles having been taken out from under it. This is the signal, and in one minute 600 lodges (on a level and beautiful prairie), which before had been strained tight and fixed, were seen waving and flapping in the wind, and in one minute more all were flat upon the ground. Their horses and dogs, of which they had a vast number, had all been secured upon the spot in readiness, and each one was speedily loaded with the burden allotted to it, and made ready to fall into the grand procession."

Painted lodges at a Sun Dance camp of the Pikunni, now called the Blackfeet Nation, of Montana, around 1906. The group of women in the foreground has gathered at the invitation of one, to help her sew a new tipi. She has chosen friends and relatives, with the work being led by one especially known for this. The hostess will feed them and give out gifts. Later she will help them in turn.

Behind them stands the Yellow Buffalo-painted lodge—one of the most ancient designs in all the Blackfoot Confederacy of Montana and Canada. For countless generations leading men and their wives went through the complex ritual of songs, prayers, and ceremonies to receive—by spiritual transfer—the rights and powers to use this design on their own family tipi covers. Several dozen such designs continue to be ceremonially transferred among the Blackfeet, who use them at Sun Dance camps and other important occasions.

*—Photograph by Walter McClintock.*

The tipi has received an added element of individuality and picturesqueness, originating, no one knows when, by the use of painted decorations in colors, representing prominent events in the history of the tribe, or of the owner, or symbolical designs of religious significance. The symbolical designs, medicine bundles, and ceremonials attached to them, which are believed to secure for their owners and their families protective power from sickness and misfortune, suggest a large and interesting field for investigation and study. These designs and the make-up of the medicine bundles were always secured through dreams, after long fasting and solitary communion with nature. They thus became, by right of discovery, the exclusive property of their owners, who might transfer them to others, but there could be no duplicates. When a painted tipi became worn out, a new one, with the same decorations, could take its place, but the owner must destroy the original, sacrificing it to the Sun by spreading it upon a lake, and sinking it beneath the water …

Painted tipis may change ownership in the fulfillment of vows made by either men or women in time of peril, or on behalf of the sick. Anyone who is willing to observe the rules of the medicine and to keep the secrets of the ceremonial can make the vow. There are, however, certain penalties, in the form of sickness or loss of property, which are believed will fall upon their owner if the ceremonial is not carefully followed. Each painted tipi has its medicine bundle composed of the skins of birds and animals, or other articles, that are used in the ceremonial of transfer and at other times. The man receiving the tipi makes payment to the owner with horses and other gifts. His relatives generally contribute, to show that they take a deep interest in the transaction and to demonstrate to the tribe that they are willing to sacrifice their property to help their clansman.

The ceremonial and feast are also given at a certain time of the year. The time for the Thunder Tipi is when the first thunder is heard in the spring, and for the Beaver Tipi when the first grass is seen—the time when the beavers are opening their winter lodges.

During a Sun Dance camp, Wolf Tail, in fulfillment of a vow to buy the Cross Stripe or Beaver Tipi, called upon Wipes-His-Eyes, the owner, and gave him a horse and a pipe as a retainer. According to the rules of the medicine, Wipes-His-Eyes could not refuse to part with the sacred tipi. The ceremonial, with full payment, took place at a later time. On the day following, when I was told of the occurrence, I visited the Cross

Part of the circular tipi camp at the North American Indian Days in Browning Montana, during the summer of 1968. Blackfeet, like many other tribal people, continue to use their traditional dwellings whenever possible. Part of their complex ceremonial life has included a series of painted lodges for untold ages. Their rituals and painted symbols have been handed down from one family to another since the stone-age buffalo times. A century of missionary and government pressure failed to destroy this powerful culture, so that scenes like this one continue across Blackfoot country.

The design on the left is called the Buffalo-head painted lodge. The black top indicates the first person using this design dreamed of it during the night. Two stripes underneath are for star constellations. The earth is shown in red paint around the bottom. The triangles above the earth represent mountain peaks. Round circles are for fallen stars. Buffalo are the lodge design's main power—represented by four buffalo skulls around the outside. The large round hump represents a prairie boulder where buffalo liked to rub—a place where hunters often found success. The tipi design began when people depended on the buffalo for most of their livelihood.

The adjoining tipi is known as the All Star-painted lodge—originating long ago in the dreams of a powerful spiritual leader among the Blackfeet. It continues to be ceremonially transferred as well.

—*Photograph by Adolf Hungrywolf.*

Stripe Tipi and saw Wolf Tail's horse tied outside, while the wife and children of Wipes-His-Eyes were mourning because they must give up their home to which they had become deeply attached, having lived in it for many years. Later in the day I saw the tipi taken down, to be pitched by Wolf Tail among the clan of the Skunks.

There were formerly men who made a specialty of painting tipis … Whenever anyone had a tipi to be painted, he gave a feast and invited his friends. After songs and prayers, all present would assist the leader chosen to do the painting. The pencils used for painting were made from buffalo bones, which were porous and readily absorbed and held the paint. A different pencil was used for each color. Willow sticks were used for ruling the lines, which were first traced out with a white liquid scraped from a hide. The paints were dug from the ground.

No Blackfoot would venture to copy the design of a painted tipi [*this was written in the 1890s but is still true in the 21st century!*], unless it had been regularly transferred to him or been received in a dream …

In nearly all of these painted tipis, there is an appropriate and logical arrangement of the decorations. There is generally, at the bottom, an encircling band of dark color representing the earth. Within this band is a row of discs called "dusty stars." The Blackfeet have given the name "dusty stars" to the puffballs that grow in circular clusters upon the prairies, because they are supposed to be meteors that have fallen from the night sky and spring up into puffballs in a single night. They call them "dusty stars" because they emit a puff of dust when pressed. Resting on this lowest band, we often find a row of rounded or pointed projections, representing rounded ridges or pointed mountain peaks. Upon the broad central space above these is portrayed the protective design of animal, bird, sacred rock, thunder trails, or other emblems, which imparts to the lodge its protective power and from which it receives its distinctive title.

Surmounting all, and including the "ears," a broad encircling band of black represents the night sky, on which are portrayed the sun and crescent moon, the constellations of the Seven Brothers and Lost Children (Great Bear and Pleiades), and a Maltese cross, the emblem of the Morning Star. This cross is also said to represent the Butterfly (or Sleep Bringer), which is believed to have great power in bringing dreams to the owner.

I was once a guest for a week in an Otter Tipi, and had the opportunity of learning the symbolic meaning of its decorations, the ceremonial belonging to it, and the pictures and signs that had been painted on the owner's body for the ceremonial of its transfer. A section of the top was painted black to represent the night sky. On it the Morning Star was represented by a yellow cross, to the centre of which was attached a sacred buffalo tail. On opposite sides of the black band the two constellations were painted in yellow clusters. A procession of otters, painted on the middle space beneath, made it an Otter Tipi and gave it the protective power promised in the dream, which originally revealed the design. At the bottom of the canvas a broad band in dark color represented the earth, and on it two parallel rows of discs were painted in yellow, to represent the "dusty stars" of the prairie.

For the ceremonial of transferring the Otter Tipi, all the painting on the face and body of the purchaser was made symbolical of the Otter. Parallel lines on both sides of his face represented otter trails. Upon his arms were painted otter paws. Over his body were otter tracks, and upon his breast a circle representing an otter lodge on the riverbank.

The painted War Tipi of Running Rabbit was of an entirely different character, being covered with picture records of tribal victories. It is an interesting fact that Indians never make records of their defeats. The War Tipi had a broad red band encircling the bottom. The top was painted black, with a red star at the back. The picture records in the central space, which were all in red, represented battles with the Crows, Sioux, Snakes, Cheyenne, and Flatheads …

A white man looking upon the inside circle of Painted Tipis, in the great encampment of the Sun Dance festival, would be impressed with their imposing array and with the spectacular effect of their novel colorings and fantastic decorations.

But it probably would never occur to him that he was looking upon pictorial representations of the tipi owner's religion. As the wearing of the crucifix is the outward sign to the world of the inward faith of many Christians, so these tipi representations of the Buffalo, Beaver, Elk, Otter, Eagle, and Antelope proclaim the belief of the Blackfeet that these sacred animals and birds have been endowed with power from the Sun …

These symbolic decorations, having a religious significance, are an ever present reminder to the family of their obligations to their tutelary medicine, and of the protection they may expect as a reward for their strict observance of its rules. Wherever the ascending smoke of their fires denotes their abode, there they piously display the symbols of their religious faith.

Walter McClintock, *The Old North Trail—Life, Legends and Religion of the Blackfeet Indians*, London, Macmillan, 1910.

A Stoney family in front of their rainbow-painted tipi, at a mountain camp near Banff, Alberta, in 1947.    —*Photograph by Nicholas Morant.*

Early reservation days on the Cree Reserve in Hobbema, Alberta, circa 1890. Horse symbols were among the most commonly used on painted lodges of the Plains tribes, such as the one seen on the second lodge here. This was a transition period for the Crees, when they still used horses and two-wheeled Red River carts to haul their seminomadic households, yet they remained settled long enough with their tipis to build solid corrals like the one in the background. The scene also shows how women generally carried firewood on their backs, and children in their blankets. —*Photograph by W. Playle.*

# Brave Buffalo Dreams of Elk

Brave Buffalo describes his dream of the elk:

"When I was about 25 years of age I was able to think for myself. I was not afraid to go into the woods, on a mountain, or in any dangerous place. At that time I was at my best in health and in worthiness, for I had conducted myself rightly in my youth, complying with all that is required of a boy and young man and living in a manner worthy of my parents and grandparents. I had a clean record when I dreamed of the elk.

"The dream came to me when I was asleep in a tent. Someone came to the door of the tent. He said he had come for me, and I arose and followed him. It was a long and difficult journey, but at last he led me to a beautiful lodge. All the surroundings were beautiful. The lodge was painted yellow outside, and the door faced the southeast. On entering the lodge I saw drawings on the walls. At the right of the entrance was a drawing of a crane holding a pipe with the stem upward, and at the left was a drawing of a crow holding a pipe with the stem downward. I could see that the occupants of the lodge were living happily and luxuriously. I was escorted to the seat of honor opposite the entrance and reached it with difficulty, as the lodge was filled with brush and I was not accustomed to making my way through thickets. (At this point the occupants of the lodge seem to have been recognized as elks.) The elks in the lodge watched me with interest and encouraged me to go on, saying they had something they wished to tell me. At last I managed to reach the seat assigned me, and when I was seated the elks rose and said they had heard that I was a great friend of the buffalo, and that they wanted me to be their friend also. They said they had tested me by requiring me to reach this difficult place, and as I had succeeded in doing so, they were glad to receive me. They then said that they were going to sing a song and wished [for] me to learn it. They sang the following song, which has no words."

Brave Buffalo said he was given various ceremonial instructions by these elk, which he afterwards always followed. Among these instructions, he was told to paint his tipi in the same manner, yellow on the outside with drawings of the crane and the crow on the inside walls, which he always did.

Frances Densmore, "Teton Sioux Music," *Bulletin of the Bureau of American Ethnology* (Bulletin 61), page 176, Smithsonian Institution, Washington, DC, 1918.

A Stoney camp of painted lodges in the Rocky Mountain foothills near Banff, Alberta, circa 1900.

—*Photograph by Edward S. Curtis.*

Two famous painted lodges used for meetings and tribal councils by the Sioux chiefs and leaders camped near Fort Yates, circa 1890. The tipi at left belonged to One Bull; the one at right to Old Bull. The drawings on both show coups and victories from the Battle of the Little Bighorn.

*—Photograph by Frank B. Fiske.*

# Origins of Tipi Designs

Most of the tipi-dwelling people of the Great Plains had occasional lodges in their midst with symbols painted on them. These were never for mere decoration, but signified instead a variety of spiritual relationships, else they declared the exploits of a brave man living inside. For those reasons, one should not copy the painting seen on another person's lodge. In fact, most Native people prided themselves in having lodges as clean and close to white as possible, made easier since reservation times by the use of white canvas, plus the limited amount of smoke from cooking and heating fires within. Tipi designs and their meanings varied among the tribes and also among individuals.

Of all the tipi-dwelling people across the plains, those of the large and warlike Blackfoot Confederacy had more lodges with painted designs than any other. Virtually all of nature's notable elements were represented by symbols among them—sun, moon, stars, earth, sky, stones, and a variety of birds and animals. These were important things in the adventuresome everyday lives of the Blackfeet. They came to the Blackfeet in dreams, gave them strength and guidance, and instructed some of them on how to paint their symbolism on lodge covers. Each one of these lodge cover paintings had its origins in a dream story, accompanied by songs and rituals that were ceremonially handed down from one family to the next, along with the rights to use the original dreamer's designs on their tipis. The faith in this complex system of spiritual tipi designs is still strong within the Blackfoot Confederacy today, with painted lodges part of every tribal encampment. None but the initiated families have traditional rights to paint such designs on their lodges, and it is considered a great disrespect for anyone else to do so.

Among the Omaha people further east on the plains, there once lived a holy man named Nikucibcan. He was considered one of the two leaders of the so-called Thunder Medicine Men who were all spiritual leaders. Around 1900 his old widow told the following story about the origins of the man's sacred lodge.

"I myself did not see him, but I have heard what was told. They say that he had a vision of the Thunder-being, so he made that rainbow which appears on his tipi. The old woman, his wife, has

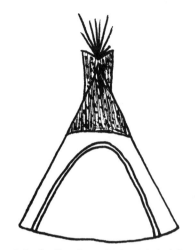

Tipi of Nikucibcan's thunder vision.

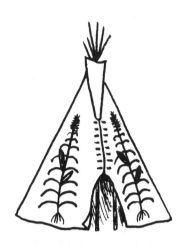

Fire Chief's cornstalk tipi.

Sacred pipe-stem tipi of Waqaga.

told this. They say that he said that the Thunder-being carried him up on high, and that the place there resembled the world. The man was regarded as very mysterious; therefore, he decorated his tent according to the pattern that he wished to make. The painted spots represent hail."

Fire Chief, a leader of the Omaha people, lived in a tipi with cornstalks painted on it. Fire Chief did not tell anyone about his dream (a common custom in the past, no one considering it proper to ask, if he did not wish to tell). His people, however, considered corn as their Mother and buffalo

as their Grandfather. It was good that a chief should have a vision of so powerful a spirit, thought his people.

Waqago (Waqaga) was a member of an Omaha clan known as the Keepers of the Pipes. According to another Omaha man, only the members of this clan painted pipe decorations upon their tipis. Among other tribes, such as the Arapaho, the keeper of a Sacred Pipe also had a pipe stem decoration on his tipi. This Omaha man made the following comments about this tipi and the pipes of his people:

"When in my childhood I saw the tents in which the people dwelt, they were of this sort. I saw the tent decorated with the pipes having feathers attached to each pipe at right angles. I saw a tent of this sort when it was occupied by Waqaga of the Pipe sub-gens. Though these pipes closely resemble peace pipes, they are made with the feathers attached to the stems at right angles. These are the pipes used in the Pipe Dance. By means of the pipes, the people made themselves that which led to chieftainship. So they regarded the sacred pipes as of the greatest importance. Even when the people were very bad, even when different tribes continued to struggle with one another, even when they shot often at one another, when some persons came forth with the peace pipes and bore them to a place between the opposing forces, carrying them all along the lines, they stopped shooting at one another. The Indians regarded the pipes as precious."

*Tipi Life Among the Omaha*, written in 1820 by the deputy agent of the Omahas, John Dougherty.

# Holy Painted Lodges

Occasionally, in connection with the power quest, the right would be given to the quester to paint his lodge in a particular manner. Among the Gros Ventre such sacred or holy painted lodges were relatively rare and were thought of very highly … Bull Lodge had been "invited" to quest for power at Baldy Butte, the highest peak in the Bear Paws. The being who gave him other powers also bestowed upon him his own lodge, with instructions how to paint it and the song to sing while it was being painted. Coming Daylight's father had a sacred lodge around the bottom of which were painted the figures of men, each figure the same and each with a feather in the head. The upper part was painted red.

John M. Cooper, "The Gros Ventres of Montana: Part II—Religion and Ritual," *The Catholic University of America Anthropological Series* 16. Washington, DC, 1956.

# Painted Tipi of the Thunder Shaman

A man who became eligible by his vision to membership in the order of Thunder shamans (could paint his) personal mystery decoration (on his) robe, or blanket (and) tent.

An old man named Dried Buffalo Skull described one such tent, or tipi, as follows:

"This tent was the personal mystery of Hupeca … of the Black Bear sub-gens (of the Omaha). After the death of Hupeca, the decoration became the property of his kinsman … The circle at the top, representing a bear's cave, is sometimes painted blue … Below the four zigzag lines (representing the lightning of different colors) are the prints of bears' paws. The lower part of the tent was blackened with ashes or charcoal. When a person had a vision of the night, or of the Thunder-being, or one of some other super terrestrial object, he blackened the upper part of his tent and a small portion on each side of the entrance."

The old chief Distant-White-Buffalo, father of the chiefs Standing Hawk and Fire Chief, had a vision of a cedar tree, which he painted on each side of his tent.

The father of Matcunaba had a vision of horses, and bequeathed to his son Matcunaba the right to decorate his tent in the style shown. The yellow was connected with the vision. When the owner dwelt in an earth lodge, the horsetail was tied to a long pole, which was thrust through the opening at the top of the lodge. So when he used his skin tent, the horsetail hung from the top of a long pole above the smoke hole.

When the Omaha dwelt near the present town of Homer, Nebraska, and Wackahi was a young child, he went out to play and fell asleep. He said that he was aroused by the sounds made by many chickens crowing and cackling. In those days there were no white people in that neighborhood; but now in that very place where Wackahi had the vision, there is a wealthy family living, and besides large herds they have a great many chickens. Wackahi painted his tent with his personal decoration (of chickens).

J. Owen Dorsey, "A Study of Siouan Cults," *Eleventh Annual Report of the Bureau of American Ethnology*, page 396, Smithsonian Institution, Washington, DC, 1890.

An early photographer recorded this Shoshoni camp back in the 1870s, when its hunters still had the option of seeking elk and moose in the mountains or going after buffalo out on the plains. These lodges were made of hides; the painted one in the foreground is the home of a tribal leader.

A young Jicarilla Apache woman stands by her tipi in 1915, wearing the cloth version of her tribe's traditional dress style. The dark painted border along the tipi's bottom was unusual among these people.

# Building
# a Tipi

An elderly woman is seen pounding wild cherries to make pemmican, in front of her partly opened lodge. The cover shows creativity in an era when extreme poverty kept the family from having a clean new lodge. Her camp was in the Rocky Mountain foothills around 1900.

# Making a Small Family Lodge

By Adolf Hungrywolf

A reference book on tipis would not be complete without explaining how they are made. For those seriously wanting to try tipi life, the best solution would be to order a tipi made by one of the tribal tipi authorities, or else from a tent and awning maker in any large city. For those wanting to make their own at home, these directions are for a ten-foot lodge, which would be considered quite small at most powwow camps, but would comfortably sleep a family of four or provide living shelter for two and still leave enough room for a fire in the middle.

A casual camping lodge of this size can be made from most any kind of cloth, although best would be a medium-weight canvas or duck. The more you plan to use the structure, the heavier your material should be. There needs to be enough of this material to end up with one solid piece measuring 10 x 20 feet. It can be bought as one piece or sewn together from many smaller sections. Another option is to buy two 10 x 10-foot canvas drop cloths at a paint store and sew these together. The canvas can be used as is, or you can coat it with a waterproofing product, although this will cause it to attract more dust and dirt.

Begin by laying out the material on a large, flat surface; then use a pencil tied to the end of a 10-foot string to mark the half circle. Use sturdy scissors or a very sharp knife to cut the material along your marked lines, as shown in the drawings, until you have the basic semicircle needed for the cover, along with a pair of triangles that will serve as smoke flaps or "ears." Sew these on as shown. Then hem the cover all the way around by folding the exposed edges back one-quarter to one-half inch. A household sewing machine works well for lighter material, while a shoemaker's machine is better for heavy canvas. The cover can also be sewn the traditional way by hand, but using nylon thread instead of sinew, along with some beeswax, a thimble, and a large needle. Wherever pieces are joined together, make sure they overlap so rainwater is shed downwards, not in. That is, an upper piece should always overlap the lower.

A double row of holes needs to be cut above the door opening on each side of the cover to hold the wooden pins that will close the tipi front. These holes need to be reinforced like buttonholes in clothing.

A piece of rope, leather thong, or strip of hemmed canvas should be sewn to the triangular piece shown between the tops of the smoke flaps. This will be used to tie the cover to the main pole for setting up the lodge.

The hemmed and rounded bottom of the tipi cover needs to have loops of hemmed canvas strips or sections of thin rope attached very firmly all around for the wooden stakes that will hold down the tipi.

A 10-foot tipi of this kind needs about a dozen poles, whereas bigger lodges require more. These poles are usually of lodgepole pine, slim, straight, peeled, dried, and at least 12 feet long. Try to find some with a bottom diameter of two or three inches and tapering toward the top. Back in nomadic times, it wasn't always possible to get a good set of poles, so the people often had to settle for whatever was at hand. The large white tipis generally seen today at powwows and other camps were an ideal back then that was seldom realized.

The front of the tipi is "buttoned up" with lacing pins usually made of willow or berry brush about pencil-thick and 10 inches long. Six or eight of these will do for a 10-foot lodge, with another two or three if you also want to button up below the doorway. Some tipi designs require these bottom buttons and others don't. The same goes for the size and shape of smoke flaps, whether they have triangular end-pockets for the poles or reinforced holes for them to go through, and whether they use three poles or four in the basic framework. These details varied by tribal custom and family preference.

A dozen or so stakes need to be made to hold down the bottom of the lodge. These are usually of willow or similar wood, an inch or more in thickness and between one and two feet long. One end needs to be sharpened to go into the ground; the other end should be beveled to take the pounding. Some stakes are nicely carved in the space between.

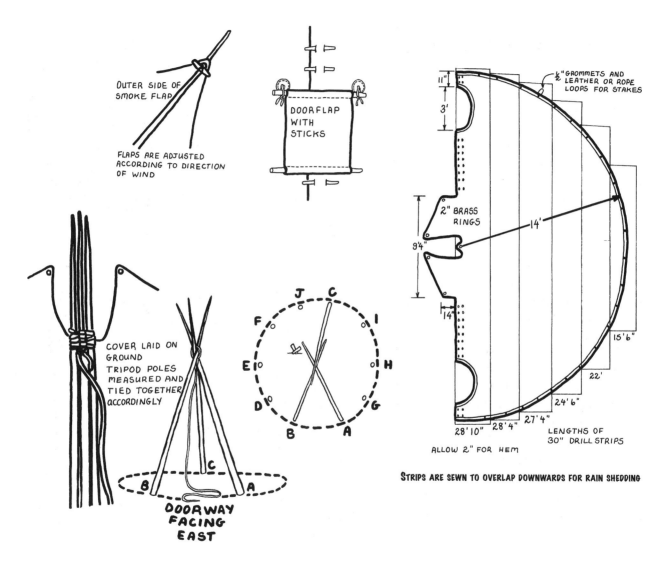

OUTER SIDE OF SMOKE FLAP

FLAPS ARE ADJUSTED ACCORDING TO DIRECTION OF WIND

DOORFLAP WITH STICKS

COVER LAID ON GROUND

TRIPOD POLES MEASURED AND TIED TOGETHER ACCORDINGLY

DOORWAY FACING EAST

½" GROMMETS AND LEATHER OR ROPE LOOPS FOR STAKES

11"

3'

2" BRASS RINGS

9'4"

14'

14"

15'6"

22'

24'6"

27'4"

28'10"

28'4"

LENGTHS OF 30" DRILL STRIPS

ALLOW 2" FOR HEM

**STRIPS ARE SEWN TO OVERLAP DOWNWARDS FOR RAIN SHEDDING**

# Setting Up a Lodge

By Gilbert Wilson

There are two ways of setting up the tipi frame, called the three-pole and the four-pole ties. The three-pole tie, used by the Mandans [*with whom Gilbert spent much time*], is perhaps the simpler.

Lay three poles on the ground as in figure 6, and bind firmly two feet from the top. The poles are set up in a tripod, figure 7, for the skeleton frame. Poles A and B, in front and spread apart, will enclose the door.

Positions of the other seven poles of the frame are shown in the ground diagram, figure 8 A, B, and C are the three poles of the skeleton frame. Poles D, E, and F on the left and G, H, and I on the right are raised in the order named. The rope or lariat L, figures 7 and 8, used for tying the skeleton frame, has been left hanging. This lariat is now drawn out through the door between poles A and B, carried around the frame, and drawn tight about the tie. The pole J in the rear of the tent is the

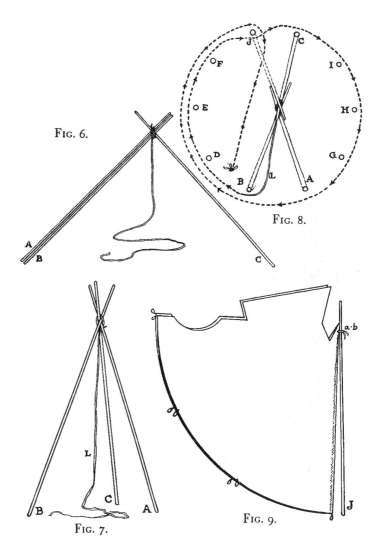

FIG. 6.

FIG. 8.

FIG. 7.

FIG. 9.

last to be placed. On this pole the canvas cover is raised.

Lay the cover on the ground, weather side up, and fold once over. Lay down the pole J, and tie the cover to it by the cord, figure 9, two feet from the top. Pole J, with the cover, is then raised in place between C and F. Before the cover is drawn, the lariat L is carried to the rear of the tent, around pole J, back into the tent again between J and C and anchored firmly to one or two pins that are driven firmly into the ground on the windward side of the fireplace. Figure 10 shows the anchored frame.

The tent cover is now drawn around the frame and laced. The loops at the lower edge of the cover are secured to the ground by tent pins driven in on a slant, shown in figure 11. The door is hung over one of the lacing pins.

Two poles are yet unused. They are raised and their upper ends are thrust into the pockets or holes of the smoke flaps. By means of these poles, the smoke flaps may be propped downwind so that the smoke may be not be driven down the smoke hole.

fig. 12

fig. 10

fig. 11

In wet weather the smoke flaps may be folded over the smoke hole by the same means. The tent, set up and ready, is shown in figure 12.

Grandma's Little Tipi. In 1968 I traveled around with my young family in search of a life in harmony with nature, visiting and staying with old-timers among several different tribes. In western Montana we spent a peaceful month along Findlay Creek on the Flathead Reservation, camped beside the little log home of Mary Ann Coombs, a noted tribal elder. Born and raised in a wilderness tipi before the tribe settled on the reservation, she was in her eighties but still bathed daily in the cold creek, regularly used her own little sweat lodge, and wore nothing but bright calico dresses, her feet protected by moccasins of smoked deer hide that she still tanned herself. She took us in as grandkids, told us to call her Grandma, then put up this little hunting tipi so that we could better experience a bit of her nature-oriented life. She insisted on putting up the lodge by herself, completing it, with inside liner and fireplace, in under an hour.

*—Photograph by Adolf Hungrywolf.*

The pins help to hold the cover down; however, during a busy period we once left a Good Medicine lodge set up all summer, fall, and winter—through wind, rain, sleet, and hail—without pinning down the bottom or anchoring the lariat, and the tipi never budged! One of the windstorms was so strong, some of the boards even flew off our barn roof.

# Inside the Lodge

By Adolf Hungrywolf

A proper lining curtain on the inside is vital to make a tipi and its fire function properly. It is best made from the same material as the lodge cover, though in a pinch it can be made from bedspreads or sheets. The inner lining has two main purposes: it provides extra insulation in cold weather, and it helps draw smoke from the lodge. This liner can be one long piece or several sheets tied side by side. A string is first rigged around the inside of the tipi from pole to pole about shoulder high. The liner or curtain is attached along its top edge by numerous thongs. The bottom is long enough to fold over a bit so that when bedding and household goods are placed on top, they will hold it down and keep outside drafts from coming in. Those drafts enter beneath the tipi cover where it is staked to the ground. Because of the snug liner, the drafts are directed upward and sucked out through the smoke hole at the tipi's top, along with smoke coming from the fire in the center. By adjusting the smoke flaps and their poles from outside, one can use the wind direction to better draw the smoke outside.

Tipi linings are often edged with bright material and decorated on their main surfaces with various designs. Notable persons liked to draw pictographs on them to show their life's exploits. The liners go all the way around from one side of the doorway to the other. For more warmth and security at night, an extra piece of liner is tied across the doorway before going to sleep.

Most tipis have pits dug in the middle for a fireplace, though the rules for some tribes forbid that, requiring the fire to be built directly on the ground. In either case, a circle of rocks usually keeps the fire within its space after all the grass and other burnable material has been cleared away. A housekeeper's skill is revealed by the way the lodge fire burns—small, warm, and smoke free.

After starting the fire with dry grass, bark, and twigs, larger pieces of wood are laid upon it, one end in and one out, so that they are like the spokes of a wheel with the flames in the center. As the sticks burn, push them farther into the fire and occasionally add new ones. In this way there will be a big pile of hot coals but only small flames, creating less smoke. A modern camper's fire has a tendency to burn the food being cooked and could easily burn visiting guests if not the whole lodge. I've seen tipis burn completely in about 10 minutes, with only charred poles left standing. When retiring for the night, pull the remaining sticks out of the fire and bury their ends in the ashes. Cover the bed of coals with ashes as well, so these will keep going all night. Blow on the coals with a pipe stem the next morning, or fan them with bird feathers, and they should come back to life. Firewood is usually kept to the left of the door, just after you enter. In good weather it can be kept outside on the ground or in a box made for that purpose.

Seating arrangements vary by tribe and family. The place of honor is at the "back" of the lodge, across the fire, opposite the doorway. Among some people this place was for the head of the household; among others it was given to distinguished guests. If the people had any medicine bundles, these were usually kept back there as well. Generally, men sat to the right as they entered, women to the left. Farthest back would be the owner and his wife—his head wife or "sits-beside-wife," if he had more than one. The first guests to arrive sat next in order, men to the right and women to the left as they entered. If an especially honored person showed up—a chief or a bundle holder—room was made for him and his wife next to the owners at the back. Unless unavoidable, others never passed between those who were seated and the fireplace, especially if they were smoking. Under no circumstances were they to pass between the fireplace and the lodge owners, especially if they had sacred bundles by them. Passing through such a "spiritual pathway" was considered worse than interrupting a speaker. Children were taught this from the start—their behavior toward guests was to be strict and with respect.

Pine boughs, ferns, and reeds from the water have all been used as tipi floor coverings, along with more recent rugs and quilts. The same material was stuffed in along the bottoms of tipi liners to help keep out the cold. This was also done with spare robes and bedding, as well as food and clothing stored in rawhide bags.

Since the arrival of metal pots in the 1600s and 1700s, tipi cooking has been centered around a tripod placed over the fire from which the pot was suspended with a metal hook and piece of chain, or by a fresh wooden hook fastened with rawhide. Sometimes two forked sticks were used instead, with a third one resting crosswise on the forks. Instead of hanging a cooking pot from this crosswise stick, it can also be used to spear pieces of meat and vegetables to be cooked over the flames. Before the coming of metal, meat was fried on the open flames, roasted on racks like those described previously, or boiled in a very basic manner. For this, a small pit was dug in the ground, then lined with a piece of fresh hide. This was filled with water, after which pieces of meat and sometimes wild vegetables were added. Hot rocks from a nearby fire were dropped into the water, bringing it quickly to a boil. When cool, the rocks were removed and replaced with others.

Back in those days, water was stored in a leaned animal paunch and hung inside from either one of the tipi poles or a tripod. Canteens were used once they were available. Metal cream cans became popular later for storing water in tipis. In modern tipi camps, many families park a camper or trailer out behind for water, cooking, or even showers. The tipi is seen as the family's spiritual connection to their ancestral past, like a practical shrine.

A small tipi camp is seen in this dramatic postcard published in Brooklyn, New York. The scant information on the back reads: "Ponca Indian Camp—Moonlight, taken in 1907 by George B. Cornish of Arkansas City, Kansas."

# Sources

## Books

Bolton, Herbert Eugene. *Coronado, Knight of Pueblos and Plains*. Albuquerque: University of New Mexico Press, 1949.

_____. *Spanish Exploration in the Southwest, 1542 to 1706 (Original Narratives of Early American History)*. New York: C. Scribner's Sons, 1916.

Daniels, Helen Sloan. *The Ute Indians of Southwestern Colorado*. Durango, CO: Durango Public Library Museum Project, 1941.

Dougherty, John. *Tipi Life Among the Omaha*. 1820.

Eastman, Charles Alexander. *Indian Boyhood*. New York: McClure, 1902.

_____. *Old Indian Days*. New York: McClure, 1907.

Hendry, Anthony. *Journal of Anthony Hendry 1754-1755*.

Keating, William H. *Journals*. 1823.

Maximilian, Prince of Wied. *Travels in the Interior of North America*. London: 1843.

McClintock, Walter. *The Old North Trail-Life, Legends and Religion of the Blackfeet Indians*. London: Macmillan, 1910.

Opler, Morris Edward. *An Apache Life-Way*. Chicago: The University of Chicago Press, 1941.

## Articles, Periodicals, and Special Reports

Bushnell, David I., Jr. "Villages of the Algonquin, Siouan, and Caddoan Tribes West of the Mississippi." *Bulletin of the Bureau of American Ethnology* 77. Smithsonian Institution, Washington, DC. (1922): 7-50.

Cooper, John M. "The Gros Ventres of Montana: Part II–Religion and Ritual." *The Catholic University of America Anthropological Series* 16. Washington, DC. 1956.

Densmore, Frances. "Teton Sioux Music." *Bulletin of the Bureau of American Ethnology* 61. Smithsonian Institution, Washington, DC. (1918): 176-448.

Dorsey, Owen J. "A Study of Siouan Cults." *Eleventh Annual Report of the Bureau of American Ethnology*. Smithsonian Institution, Washington, DC. (1890): 396-487.

Fletcher, Alice C., & Francis La Flesche. "The Omaha Tribe." *Twenty-seventh Annual Report of the Bureau of American Ethnology*. Smithsonian Institution, Washington, DC. (1905-1906): 337.

Mandelbaum, David "The Plains Cree." *Anthropological Papers of the American Museum of Natural History* 37. New York. 1940.

Parsons, Elsie Clews. "Kiowa Tales." *American Folklore Society Memoir* 22. New York. (1929): 138.

Teit, James A. "The Salishan Tribes of the Western Plateaus." *Forty-fifth Annual Report of the Bureau of American Ethnology*. Smithsonian Institution, Washington, DC. 1927.

Turney-High, Harry Holbert. "The Flathead Indians of Montana." *Memoirs of the American Anthropological Association* 48. Menasha, Wisconsin. 1937.

Wilson, Gilbert L. "Agriculture of the Hidatsa Indians—An Indian Interpretation." *Studies in Social Sciences*, no. 9. University of Minnesota, Minneapolis. (1917): 118.

____. "The Horse and Dog in Hidatsa Culture." *Anthropological Papers of the American Museum of Natural History* XV, II. New York. (1924): 243-307.

# Index

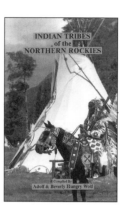
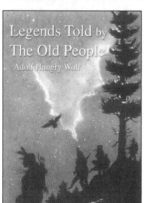